Published by Aperitifs Publishing Company
Santa Rosa, California

Original manuscript by Tim Higgins
Manuscript purchased & rewritten by John C. Burton
Copyright: October 2024

Compiled & Published by John C. Burton,
Johncburton@msn.com - 707-523-1611

ISBN: 978-1-7324530-9-8
Library of Congress Number: 2024921910
Printed in the United States of America

All rights reserved. No part of this book may be reproduced or transformed in any form or by any means, electronic or mechanical, including photocopying, recording or by any information storage and/or retrieval system without permission in writing from the publisher.

I, John C. Burton, on September 23, 2022, purchased the contents, material and rights to this publication from Tim Higgins of Jackson, California.

FRONT COVER ACKNOWLEDGEMENTS

NEW ALMADEN VICHY WATER CALIFORNIA	Eric McGuire
BAY CITY SODA WORKS S.F.	John C. Burton
JOHN S. BAKER	Mike Southworth
BORDWELL MINERAL WATER	Mike Southworth
LYNDE & PUTMAN MINERAL WATER SAN FRANCISCO CAL A	John C. Burton

BACK COVER ACKNOWLEDGEMENTS

CALIFORNIA NATURAL SELTZER WATER	Richard Siri
EAGLE (Owen Casey & James Kelly)	Rick Siri
DITZ & ELLERKAMP SODA WORKS SAN FRANCISCO	Eric McGuire
CRYSTAL SODA WATER (Benicia Glass)	John C. Burton
B & G SAN FRANCISCO	John C. Burton

RECENT ACKNOWLEDGEMENTS

On the next page you will find original acknowledgements from Tim Higgins book "EARLY SODA & MINERAL WATER BOTTLES OF THE OLD WEST." I purchased the rights to the book and have tried to take it to the next level by adding additional bottles. I have also incorporated information from Peck & Audie Markota's publications with permission from their daughter, Jeanne Deschamps.

With that being said, I want to thank Rick Siri, Richard Siri, Eric McGuire, Dr. Tom Jacobs and Mike Southworth for their recent contributions in addition those individuals listed on the next page.

BOTTLE VALUE

Values vary so much regarding color, condition, rarity and what you choose to pay & what the seller will accept. So, I placed a $ _____ with each bottle for you to record what either you paid, sold or feel the current value of the particular bottle is worth.

ACKNOWLEDGEMENTS

This page of acknowledgements is for the revised 2020 edition. I would like to thank American Bottle Auctions and Glass Works Auctions for many of the photos. And a special thanks to Max Bell for the use of his research regarding the Golden Gate Soda. Also, to Mike Southworth for upgrading some of the bad pictures with some photos from his superb collection of western sodas. Warren Friedrich supplied the updated information on the earliest pontiled sodas.

DAN BELL, AUBURN CA.
MAX BELL, AUBURN CA.
JOHN C. BURTON, SANTA ROSA, CA.
RON CECIL, STOCKTON, CA.
TOM CHAPMAN, BIG PINE, CA.
WARREN FRIEDRICH, GRASS VALLEY, CA.
RICK HALL, SAN DIEGO, CA.
DOUG HANSON, PALO CEDRO, CA.
MIKE HENNESS, IONE, CA.
FRED HOLABIRD, RENO, NV.
DONALD KING, BENICIA, CA.
ANDREW KOUTSOUKOS, SAN RAFAEL, CA.
RICK LINDGREN, MARTINEZ, CA.
TOM QUINN, BENICIA, CA.
JAMES QUINN, BENICIA
CY ROLLINS, GOODYEARS BAR, CA.
RICK SIMI, DOWNIEVILLE, CA.
MIKE SOUTHWORTH, UPLAND, CA.
JEFF WICHMAN, SACRAMENTO, CA.

Another special thanks to the bottle diggers and collectors who inspired Peck and Audie Markota to research and write great books. It has been the go-to source for information on Western Sodas since the day it was completed. It has been an honor for me to update it.

CALIFORNIA MINERAL WATER & SODA BOTTLES

AETNA MINERAL SPRINGS

Location:	Pope Valley
Face:	**AETNA** **MINERAL WATER**
Reverse:	**AETNA** **MINERAL WATER**
Bottom:	Blank
Date:	1886 – 1905
Rarity:	Common
Proprietor:	Chancellor Hartson
Address:	Napa Springs
City:	San Francisco, Ca.
Value:	$ _____
	John Burton Collection

1886–1887	Aetna Mineral Springs A. F. Learned Agent, 757½ Howard
1887–1888	A. T. Cooper Agent, 757½ Howard
1888–1889	Owens & Bartlett Agents, 513 Montgomery Street Warehouse 57 Clay, Tel. 536
1889-1899	L.D. Owen President John J. O'Brien Secretary 106-108 Drumm, Tel. 536
1899-1900	John J. O'Brien President Lin & Louis Klee Sole Agents 619 Montgomery, Tel. Main 1729
1900-1901	Louis Klee & Co. Sole Agents U.S. 604-608 Bryant Street
1901-1902	Baumgarten & Co. Sole Agents U. S. 604-608 Bryant Street
1902-1903	No listing
1903-1904	Aetna Mineral Water Agency No. 7 Tenth Street
1904-1905	Aetna Mineral Water Agency Hilbert Mercantile Co. Agents 213 Market Street
1905	Aetna Mineral Water Agency 140 Second Street
1906	Earthquake

AETNA MINERAL SPRINGS

Location:	Pope Valley
Face:	AETNA MINERAL WATER TRADE MARK REGISTERED
Reverse:	AETNA MINERAL WATER TRADE MARK REGISTERED
Bottom:	AETNA
Date:	1886 - 1905
Rarity:	Common
Proprietor:	Chancellor Hartson
Address:	Napa Springs
City:	San Francisco, Ca.
Value:	$ _____
	John Burton Collection

AETNA MINERAL SPRINGS

Location:	Pope Valley
Face:	**AETNA**
	SODA WATER
Reverse:	**NATURAL**
	MINERAL WATER
Bottom:	Blank
Date:	1886 – 1905
Rarity:	Obtainable
Proprietor:	Chancellor Hartson
Address:	Napa Springs
City:	San Francisco, Ca.
Value:	$ _____
	John Burton Collection

AMERICAN FLAG MINERAL WATER

Location: San Francisco
Face: AMERICAN

              MINERAL WATER
                   S.F.

Reverse: Blank
Bottom: Blank
Date: 1899 – 1906
Rarity: Rare
Proprietor: James J. Rooney & Ernest E. Zimmerman
1899 – 1905   924 Bryant Street
1905 – 1915   2485 Bryant Street
Value $ _____

ASTORG MINERAL WATER
AZULE SELTZER SPRINGS
Location: Cobb Valley Lake County

Face:	**ASTORG**
	MINERAL
	WATER
Reverse:	Blank
Bottom:	Blank
Date:	1896-1906
Proprietor:	Alphonse Astorg
Address:	Astorg's Butcher Shop
	108 Fifth Street
Color:	Aqua
Value	$ _____
	Richard Siri Collection

AZULE SELTZER SPRINGS

Location:	Santa Clara 12 Miles Southwest of San Jose
	Originally known as Mills Seltzer Springs
Face:	AZULE
	SELTZER
	SPRINGS
Reverse:	TRADE 🐻 MARK
Bottom:	Blank
Date:	1885 – 1890
Rarity:	Scarce
Value	$ _____

B	(Charles Belden)
Location:	Marysville & Stockton
Face:	B
Reverse:	Blank
Bottom:	Blank
Date:	1871 – mid 1880's
Proprietor:	Charles Belden
Rarity:	Common

MARYSVILLE

1870-1875	Charles Belden
	Corner Second & Virgin Alley
1875-1885	Lyman Belden (Charles's brother)
	Corner Second & Virgin Alley
1885 – 1900's	Charles Belden
	Second Street between B & C Streets

STOCKTON

1870-1895	Charles Belden
	Corner Weber & San Joaquin Street
1895-1900's	Charles Belden & S.B. Huskins
	303 East Weber Street
Value	$ _____

BABB & CO.

Location:	San Francisco
Face:	BABB & CO.
	SAN FRANCISCO
	CAL.
Recverse:	Blank
Bottom:	Blank
Date:	1852-1854
Rarity:	Scarce
Proprietor:	Jeffries Babb
Address:	380 Dupont Street
Value:	$ _____

ADDITIONAL COLORS OF BABB & CO. BLOB TOP BOTTLES

HENRY BADER & CO.
X L C R SODA WORKS

Location:	San Francisco
Panels:	S. F.
(Vertical)	H. BADER & Co.
	PENALTY
	FOR SELLING
	THIS BOTTLE
	XLCR
	SODA WORKS
	738 BROADWAY
	S.F.
Reverse:	Blank
Bottom:	Blank
Date:	1861 – 1872
Rarity:	Extremely Rare
Proprietor:	Louis & Peter Bader
	525 Vallejo Street
	Louis & Henry Bader
	738 Broadway
	Christian & Henry Bader
	738 Broadway
City:	San Francisco, Ca
Value:	$ _____
.	Eric McGuire collection

JOHN S. BAKER

Location:	Sacramento
Panels:	JOHN S. BAKER
	MINERAL WATERS
	THIS BOTTLE
	IS NEVER SOLD
Bottom:	Blank
Date:	c.1853-1857
Rarity:	Citron Off the charts
	Aqua & Green Extremely Rare
Embossing	Two variants large & small font
Proprietor:	John S. Baker
Value:	$ _____
	Mike Southworth Collection

WHERE HAVE YOU EVER SEEN JOHN S. BAKER IN THIS COLOR?
Mike Southworth Collection
Left Image: THIS BOTTLE/IS NEVER SOLD
Right Image: MINERAL WATERS

JOHN S. BAKER
Mike Southworth Collection

BAY CITY SODA WORKS

Face:	**BAY CITY SODA WORKS**
	Co.
	S.F.
Reverse:	**STAR**
Bottom:	Blank
Date:	1871 – 1878
Corporation:	James McEwen president
Address(s)	89 Stevenson Street
	1878 – 1881
	110 Tyler Street
	1881 – 1895
	110-112 Golden Gate Ave.
	1895 – 1897
	116 - 118 Golden Gate Ave
	1897- 1906
	117 – 123 Hyde Street
	1907 – 1913
	320 Fell Street
City:	San Francisco, Ca.
	Value $ _____
	John Burton Collection

BAY CITY VARIOUS COLORS

BELFAST

Location: San Francisco
Face: **BELFAST
TRADE/B MARK
GINGER ALE CO.
S.F.**

Reverse: Blank
Bottom: Blank
Date:
1877-1881 John & Alexander Chambers &
Thomas Pyne 1637 Howard Street
1881-1888 Thomas Pyne 145 Valencia Street
1888- 1921 Frederick & Richard Steimke
Corner Octavia & Union Streets
Rarity: Rare
Value: $_____

BELFAST (Vertical)
Location: San Francisco
Face: THE BELFAST
GINGER ALE CO.
SAN FRANCISCO
Date: Approximately 1877-1881
Rarity: Rare
Value: $ _____

B & G.	**TYPE 1 BOTTLE**
Location:	San Francisco
Face:	B. & G.
	SAN FRANCISCO
Reverse:	SUPERIOR
	MINERAL WATER
Bottom:	Blank
Date:	1852 - 1854
	Bache & Grotjan Druggist
	213 Washington St.
	1854 – 1855
	Grogan & Co. Druggist
	1856
	Grogan & Co. Drug Brokers
	112 California Street
City:	San Francisco, Ca.
Value:	$ _____
	John C. Burton Collection

		TYPE 2 BOTTLE
B & G.		
Location:	San Francisco	
Face:	B. & G.	
	SAN FRANCISCO	
Reverse:	SUPERIOR	
	MINERAL WATER	
Bottom:	Blank	
Date:	1852 - 1854	
	Bache & Grotjan Druggist	
	213 Washington St.	
	1854 – 1855	
	Grogan & Co. Druggist	
	1856	
	Grogan & Co. Drug Brokers	
	112 California Street	
City:	San Francisco, Ca.	
Value:	$ _____	
	John C. Burton Collection	

E. L. BILLINGS

Location:	Sacramento
Face:	E. L. BILLINGS
	SAC. CITY
Reverse:	GEYSER SODA
Bottom:	Blank
Date:	1872 - 1879
Proprietor:	Ephraim L. Billings
Address:	417 K Street
City:	Sacramento, Ca.
Value:	$ _____

ADDITIONAL E. L. BILLINGS SAC CITY COLORS

BOLEY & Co.   Type 1 Blob Top

Location:	Sacramento
Face:	BOLEY & Co.
	SAc CITY CAL
Reverse:	UNION GLASS WORKS
	PHILADA.
Bottom:	Open Pontil & Open Pontil Mark
Date:	1850-1862
Color:	Cobalt
Rarity:	Iron Pontil Scarce
	Open Pontil Extremely Scarce
Variant:	Some have reverse slugged out
	UNION GLASS WORKS/PHILADA
Proprietor:	Addison & Lafayette Boley
Address:	1850-1853 Front Street between H & I
	1854-1855 On Levee above Water Works
	1856 Above Water Works
	1857 Near Water Works
	1858 Near the Station House
	1861-1862 Corner of H Street
Value	$ _____

BOLEY & Co. Type 2 Blob Top
Location: Sacramento
Face: BOLEY & Co.
            SAc CITY CAL

Reverse: UNION GLASS WORKS
                PHILADA.
Bottom: Open Pontil & Open Pontil Mark
Date: 1850-1862
Color: Cobalt
Rarity: Iron Pontil Scarce
            Open Pontil Extremely Scarce
Variant: Some have reverse slugged out
            UNION GLASS WORKS/PHILADA
Proprietor: Addison & Lafayette Boley
Address: 1850-1853 Front Street between H & I
            1854-1855 On Levee above Water Works
            1856 Above Water Works
            1857 Near Water Works
            1858 Near the Station House
            1861-1862 Corner of H Street
Value $ _____

BONANZA MINERAL WATER

Location:	Mendocino County
Face:	G. M. HENDERSON
	BONANZA
	MINERAL WATER
	MENDOCINO
	CAL.
Reverse:	Blank
Bottom:	Blank
Rarity:	Scarce
Date:	1890 - 1892
Proprietor:	George M. Henderson
Address:	Two miles from Seigler's springs
City:	Mendocino, Ca.
Value:	$ _____
	John C. Burton Collection

BORDWELL MINERAL WATER
Location: Placer County or Oroville
Face: BORDWELL & CO
        MINERAL WATER

Reverse: BORDWELL & CO
         MINERAL WATER
Bottom: Blank
Date: 1852
Rarity: Extremely Rare
Proprietor: John Bordwell
City:
Value: $ _____
            Mike Southworth Collection

There is evidence that John Bordwell & W.E. Deamer were in business together in Oroville in 1857-1858. Two of these bottles were dug under the Old Shanghai Bar and Restaurant in Auburn. Information from Mike Southworth.

From The Collection of Mike Southworth

North Californian (Or... • 25 Apr 1856

PROTECT HOME INDUSTRY.—Messrs. DEAMER & BORDWELL, Soda Manufacturers, are always on hand, always on the square, have their families among us, make the best article of Soda, Ale, and Porter, (this we know for we have had a taste) drive a good team, and are good fellows generally, and should be patronized in preference to strangers. Let our saloon keepers bear this in mind.

The North Californian (Or... • 01 Aug 1856, Fr

DEAMER & BORDWELL,
MANUFACTURERS OF
MINERAL WATER, ALE, AND PORTER.
The patronage of the citizens of Butte County is respectfully solicited.

MINERAL WATER.—Messrs. Bordwell & Deamer, the enterprising manufacturers of this healthful beverage, supplied this office with large quantities of the liquid during those hot days, when it was most acceptable.

SODA.—We neglected yesterday to acknowledge the receipt of a couple of dozen bottles of soda, from the manufactory of Messrs. Bordwell & Deamer, Robinson street.

BREIG & SCHAFER

Location:	San Francisco
Face:	(Fish)
	BREIG & SCHAFER
	S. F.
Reverse:	Blank
Bottom:	Blank
Date:	1879 – 1890
Rarity:	Aqua Scarce
	Green Rare
Proprietor:	John Breig & George Schafer
Address:	38 Hayes Street
City:	San Francisco, Ca.
Value:	$ _____
	John Burton Collection

W. H. BURT

Location:	San Francisco
Face:	W. H. BURT
	SAN FRANCISCO
Reverse:	Blank
Bottom:	Iron Pontil Mark
Rarity:	Scarce
Date:	1852
	William H. Burt
Address	1618 Powell Street
	1862-1863
	Westside Mason Between
	Broadway & Vallejo
	1863-1864
	1513 Mason
	1864-1865
	209 Tehama Street
City:	San Francisco, Ca.
Value	$ _____
	Rick Siri Collection

Cammet & Buffum sold their soda works located on Stafford Street H. William H. Burt.

CALIFORNIA SELTZER WATER

Location:	Cloverdale
FACE:	CALIFORNIA SELTZER WATER
Reverse:	(Bear) H. & G.
	Bottom: Blank
Date:	1875 – 1885
Rarity:	With Grass Under Bear Extremely Rare
	Without Grass Under Bear Rare
Proprietor:	Martin Heller & William T. Garrett
Address:	
City:	Cloverdale, Ca.
Value:	$ _____
	Richard Siri Collection

CALIFORNIA NATURAL SELTZER SPRINGS

Location:	Cloverdale
FACE:	CALIFORNIA
	NATURAL
	SELTZER WATER
Reverse:	(Bear)
	H. & G.
	Bottom: Blank
Date:	1875 – 1880
Rarity:	With Grass Under Bear Extremely Rare
	Without Grass Under Bear Rare
Proprietor:	Martin Heller & William T. Garrett
Address:	
City:	Cloverdale, Ca.
Value:	$ _____
	Richard Siri Collection

CALIFORNIA NATURAL SELTZER WATER

Location:	Cloverdale
Face:	CALIFORNIA
	NATURAL
	SELTZER WATER
Reverse:	(Bear) H & G
Bottom:	Blank
Date:	1875 – 1885`
Rarity:	With Grass Under Bear Extremely Rare
	Without Grass Rare
Proprietor:	Martin Heller & William Garratt
Address:	518 Market Street
City:	San Francisco, Ca.
Value:	$ _____
	Richard Siri Collection

ADDITIONAL CALIFORNIA NATURAL SELTZER WATER BOTTLES

CALIFORNIA NATURAL SELTZER WATER

CALIFORNIA SODA WORKS

Location:	San Francisco
Face:	CALIFORNIA SODA WORKS
	(Branches)
	H. FICKEN
	S.F.
Reverse:	EAGLE
Bottom:	Blank
Date:	1878 – 1879
Rarity:	Aqua Rare
	Blue Scarce
	Apple Green Extremely Rare
Proprietor:	Henry Ficken
Address:	723 Turk Street
City:	San Francisco, Ca.
Value:	$ _____

Henry Ficken was listed as a driver for Eureka Soda Works in 1880-1881

ADDITIONAL HENRY FICKEN COLORED BOTTLES

C & K – EAGLE SODA WORKS SACRAMENTO
(Owen Casey & James Kelly)

Location:	Sacramento
Face:	C. & K.
	EAGLE WORKS
	SAC. CITY
Reverse:	Blank
Bottom:	Blank
Date:	1858 – 1860
Rarity:	Scarce
Proprietor:	Owen Casey & James Kelly Importers & Dealers in liquors, wine, brandies, wholesale and retail soda bottling.
Address:	109 K Street Sacramento
Date:	1860-1866
	Owen Casey & James Kelly Soda Factory 107 K Street
City:	Sacramento, Ca.
Value	$ _____

C & R. – EAGLE WORKS SACRAMENTO
(Casey & James Kelly??)

Location:	Sacramento
Face:	C. & R.
	EAGLE WORKS
	SAC. CITY
Reverse:	Blank
Bottom:	Blank
Date:	1860's
Rarity:	Vary Rare
Proprietor:	Owen Casey & James Kelly??
Address	109 K Street
City:	Sacramento, Ca.
Value	$ _____

Markota believes that this bottle was a mistake regarding the initials of C & R and should have been C & K instead. At this time period many bottles were misspelt.

OWEN CASEY- EAGLE SODA WORKS SACRAMENTO

Location:	Sacramento
Face:	OWEN CASEY
	EAGLE SODA
	WORKS
Reverse:	SAC. CITY
Bottom:	Blank
Date:	1867 – 1868
	Owen Casey & J. W. Schoonmaker
	1869
	Owen Casey & Andrew Crozier
	1870 Proprietor of Jockey Club Saloon
	Located at 167 K Street
	1870 - 1871
	Owen Casey Liquor Dealer
	1871 S. Crown Soda Employee
Rarity:	Aqua Common
	Blue Semi-Common
	Apple Green Rare
Proprietor:	Owen Casey
Address:	50 K Street
City:	Sacramento, Ca.
Value:	$ _____
	John C. Burton Collection

OWEN CASEY EAGLE SODA WORKS

CASSIN'S ENGLISH AERATED WATERS

Location:	San Francisco
Face:	CASSIN'S ENGLISH AERATED WATERS
Reverse:	Blank
Bottom:	Curved
Date:	1872
Proprietor:	Cassin Brothers
Address:	522 Front Street
Rarity:	Rare
Value:	$ _____

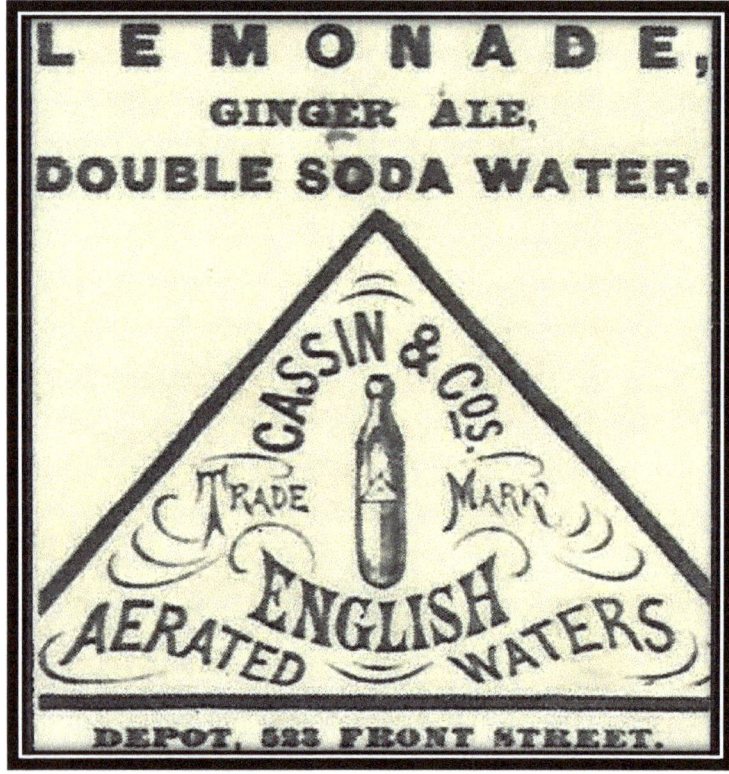

C C & B
(Crowell, Crane & Brigham)

Location:	San Francisco
Face:	**C C & B**
	SAN FRANCISCO
Reverse:	**SUPERIOR**
	MINERAL WATER
Bottom:	Blank
Date:	1856 – 1858
Rarity:	Extremely Rare
Proprietor:	Cromwell, Crane & Brigham
Address:	151 Commercial Street
City:	San Francisco, Ca.
Value:	$ _____
	Max Bell Collection

CROWELL, CRANE & BRIGHAM

Crowell, Crane & Brigham located at 131 Commercial Street in San Francisco are listed as being in business from 1856-1858. When this bottle was blown it appears as if it was blown from an altered B & G mug base mold.

The majority of mug base sodas have "Union Glass Works" on the reverse. This bottle is embossed on the reverse "Superior/Mineral Water" above "Union Glass Works."

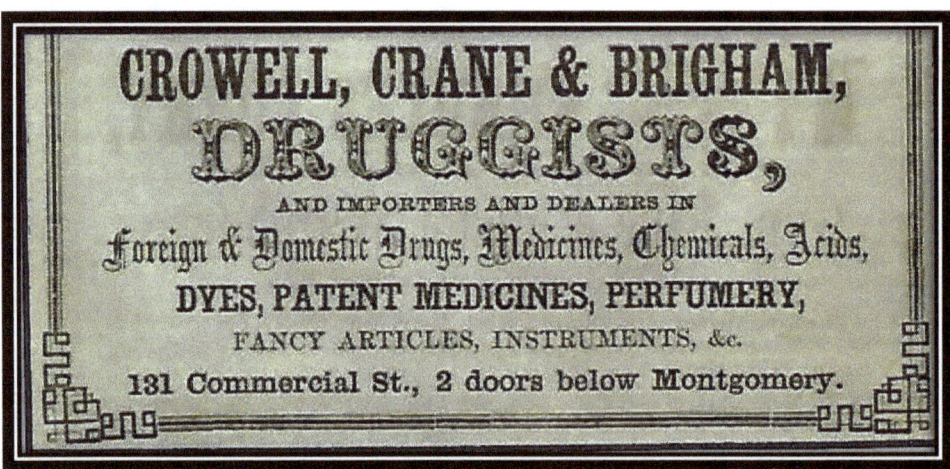

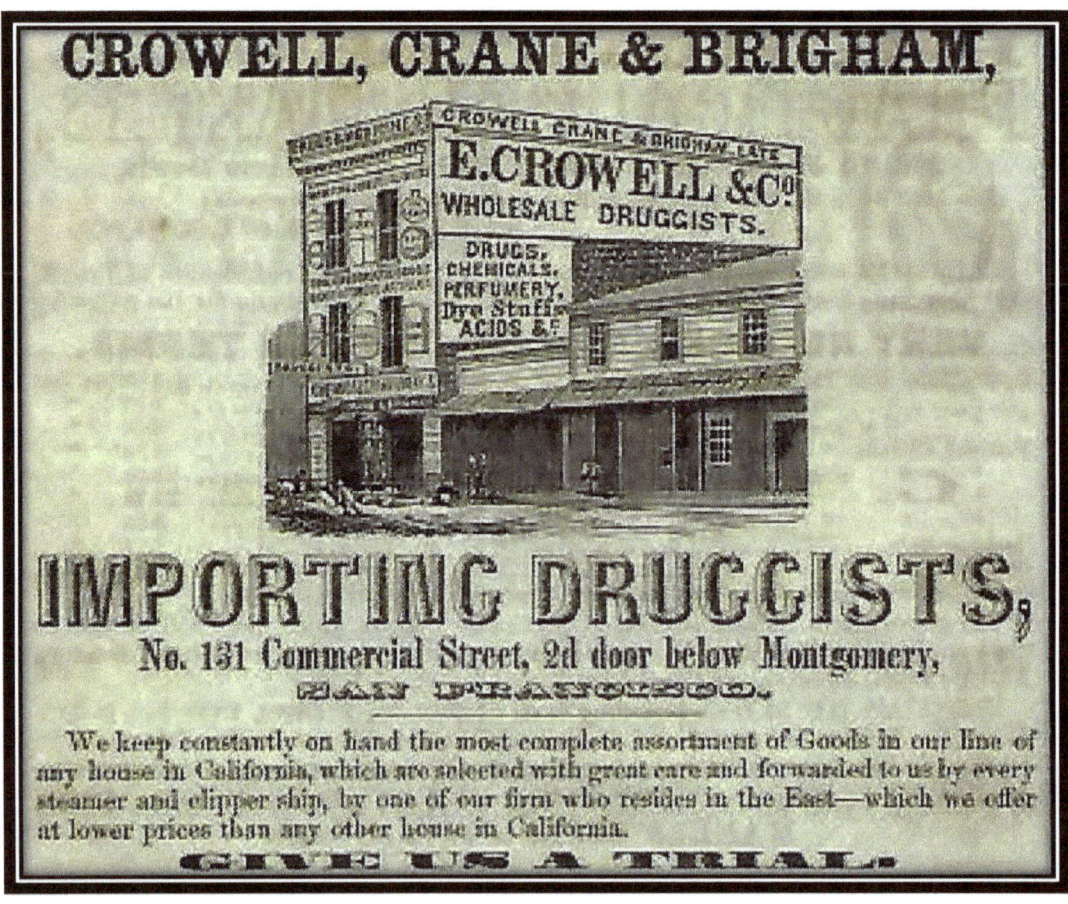

CHAMPAGNE MEAD

Location:	San Francisco
Face:	CHAMPAGNE
(Vertical)	MEAD
Reverse:	Blank
Bottom:	Blank
Date:	1871 – 1872
Rarity:	Aqua Rare
	Blue Very rare
	Apple Green Extremely Rare
Proprietor:	William Gass,
	John Bolland & W. H. Emerson
Address:	114 Turk Street
City:	San Francisco, Ca.
Value:	$ _____

PATENT, PATENT, WHO'S GOT THE PATENT?

Two separate individuals (Companies) applied for a U. S. Patent on the name "CHAMPAGNE MEAD" In California.

April 5, 1870, Frank Kenyon & Co. applied for a patent on the name "Champagne Mead."

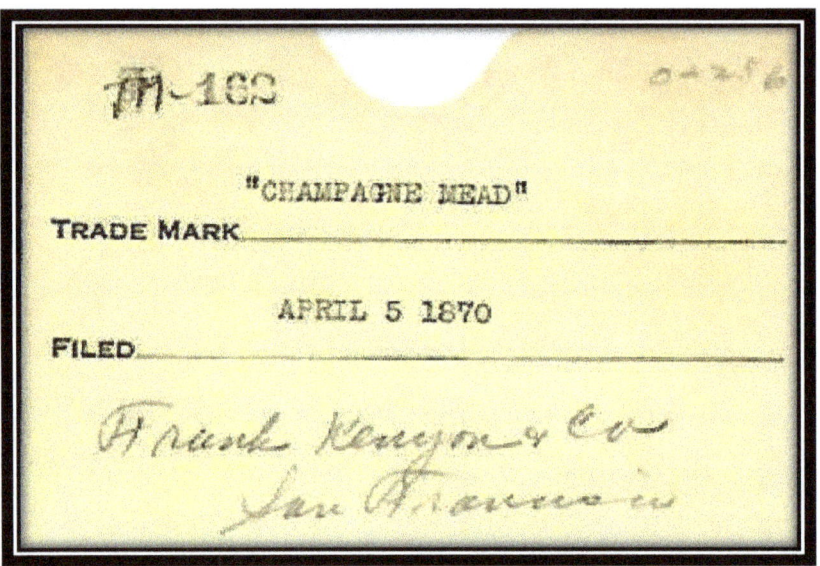

August 16, 1870, Asher S. Taylor patented with the U. S. Patent Office," Improved Beverage called Champagne Mead." Asher Taylor had a pontiled soda bottle with his name on it in the 1850's.

The April 6, 1870 edition of the Sacramento Daily Union states that Frank Kenyon & Co. trade marked the name "Champane Mead."

The only public listing in San Francisco was 1871-1872, Gass & Co., William C. Gass, John Boland and W. H. Emerson, Champagne Mead Works, 114 Turk Street.

May 27, 1870 the Sacramento Daily Union listed an advertisement Thos. Davidson, agent at 134 K Street, Sacramento.

> **WANTED.**
>
> EVERY MAN, WOMAN AND CHILD should know that I am introducing the celebrated PATENT BEVERAGE, CHAMPAGNE MEAD, and that there is neither ACID nor Marble Dust used in its composition, and that it should not be mentioned in connection with a certain so-called Mead foisted upon this market by parties interested in Soda Water.
>
> THOS. DAVIDSON, Agent.
>
> Depot, 134 K street.   my24-1w3p*

August 20, 1870, a dissolution notice was filed in the Sacramento Daily Union between Frank Kenyon, W. C. Gass & W. Fowler. The notice was filed four days after Asher Taylor applied for his patent.

> **DISSOLUTION NOTICE** — THE Co-partnership heretofore existing between F. KENYON, W. C. GASS and W. W. FOWLER, under the style of Kenyon, Gass & Co., carrying on the manufacturing of Champagne Mead and Calisaya Bitters, in this city, is dissolved by mutual consent, this day; F. Keynor and W. W. Fowler having disposed of their interest to W. C. Gass & Co., who will continue the business at the Manufactory, 114 Turk street.
>
> All claims due the late firm are payable to W. C. Gass & Co., who will settle all the bills of the late firm, with the exception of a certain reserve held by the firm.
>
> FRANK KEYON,
> W. C. GASS.
> W. W. FOWLER.
>
> San Francisco, Cal., August 29, 1870.   au31

ADDITIONAL CHAMPAGNE MEAD BOTTLES

CHASE & COMPANY MINERAL WATER – SAN FRANCISCO

Location:	San Francisco
Face:	CHASE & CO. MINERAL WATER SAN FRANCISCO CAL.
Reverse:	Blank
Bottom:	Iron Pontil Mark
Date:	1852 Jorgensen & Frederick Chase Dissolved partnership. Chase & Co. became successors to Lynde & Putnam water manufactures located at Broadway near Kearny. 1854-1855 Located at Vallejo & Pinckney Streets 1856 Able Cudworth purchased company
Rarity:	Scarce
Proprietor:	James & Frederick Chase Able W. Cudworth (1856)
City:	San Francisco, Ca.
Value:	$ _____

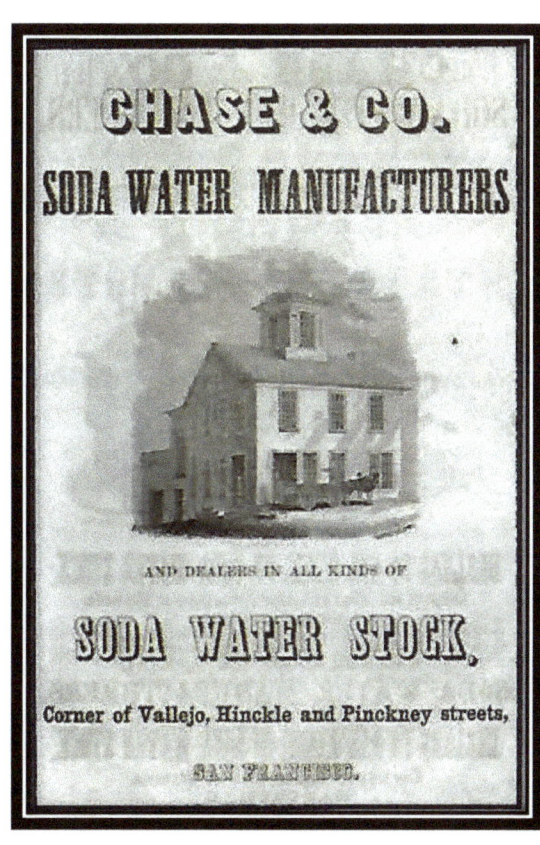

CHASE & COMPANY – SAN FRANCISCO, MARYSVILLE & STOCKTON

Face:	**CHASE & CO.**
	MINERAL WATER
	SAN FRANCISCO
	STOCKTON
	MARYSVILLE
Reverse:	Blank
Bottom:	Iron Pontil mark
Dates:	**STOCKTON**
	1853–1854
	Common & Commerce Streets
	1854-1855 Chase & Co. Soda Factory Market & Commerce Streets
Proprietor:	1856
	J. D. Vaughn proprietor
Address:	Market & Commercial Streets
	MARYSVILLE
	1853-1854
	Sixth & Alley above A Street
	1854-1855
	Corner 6th & A Streets
Rarity:	Very rare
City:	Stockton, Ca
Value:	$ _____

R. L. & P. Brader took over Chase & Company in 1858 Locating at 165 Yuba Alley in Marysville.

Frederick Chase went to work as a clerk for the Sitka Ice Company and returned to bottling soda water and vinegar in 1860. His company was listed as Chase & Co. 165 Yuba Alley, Marysville the again Chase & Co. at No. 1 Third Street, Marysville.

CLASSEN & COMPANY

Location:	San Francisco
Face:	CLASSEN & Co.
	SAN
	FRANCISCO
Reverse:	PACIFIC
	SODA
	WORKS
Bottom:	Blank
Date:	1863 – 1868
Rarity:	Aqua Semi Common
	Apple Green Rare
	Blue Rare
Proprietor:	Milton J. Classen & John F. Rohe
Address:	115 Jesse Street
City:	San Francisco, Ca.
Value:	$ _____
	Rick Siri Collection

ADDITIONAL CLASSEN – THREE DIFFERENT REVERSE BOTTLES

PACIFIC SODA – CLASSEN & CO.

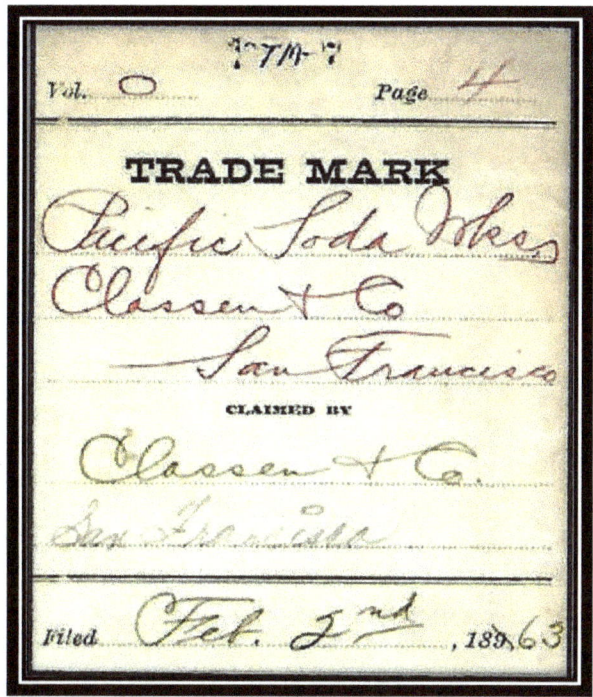

CLASSEN & CO. SPARKLING (Sparkling Cider)

Location:	San Francisco
Face:	Blank
On Shoulder	**CLASSEN & CO.**
	(Anchors)
	SPARKLING
Reverse:	Blank
Bottom:	Blank
Date:	1864 – 1868
Rarity:	Aqua, Blue, Cobalt & Green All very rare
Proprietor:	Milton J. Classen & John F. Rohe
Address:	115 Jesse Street
City:	San Francisco
Value:	$ _____
	Rick Siri Collection

CLASSEN & CO. SPARKLING

COLUMBIA SODA WORKS

Location:	San Francisco & Oakland
Face:	COLUMBIA
	SODA
	WORKS
	S.F.
Reverse:	Seated Liberty
	C. C. DALL
Bottom:	Blank
Date:	SAN FRANCISCO
	1879 – 1879
	733 Broadway
	OAKLAND
	1880-1881
	754 Clay Street
Rarity:	Aqua Rare
	Blue Rare
	Apple Green Very rare
	Amber Extremely Rare
Proprietor:	Christopher C. Dall
Value:	$ _____

COLUMBIA MINERAL WATER
Location: San Francisco
Face: **COLUMBIA**
                  NAPA
         TRADE (Eagle) MARK
                  COUNTY
             MINERAL WATER
Reverse: Blank
Bottom: Blank
Date: 1892-1894
                G. L. Abell
Address: Depot 641 Mission Street
City: San Francisco
Value: $ _____

COLUMBIA – R & H

Location:	Columbia, Tuolumne County
Face:	R & H.
	COLUMBIA
	CAL.
Reverse:	Blank
Bottom:	Blank
Rarity:	Very Rare
Date:	1852-1854
	Albert Holton
	1854 -1860
	Albert Holton & VanRennselaer Raymond
	1860-1864
	VanRennselaer Raymond
City:	Columbia, Ca.
Value:	$ _____

COLUSA

Location:	Colusa, Colusa County
Face:	P. & B. COLUSA CALA.
Reverse:	Blank
Bottom:	Blank
Rarity:	Extremely Rare
Date:	1877-1885 Jonathon Poulson 1885-1887 T. H. Polly 1887-1888 T. H. Polly & Rankin Blackburn 1888-1900's Rankin Blackburn 1900's T. F. Phillips
Address:	Third & Market Street
City:	Colusa, Ca.
Value	$ _____

B. F. CONNOLLY

Location:	Petaluma
Face:	CONNOLLY & Bto.
Reverse:	GEYSER SODA
Bottom:	Blank
Rarity:	Semi Rare
Date:	1872 - 1873
Proprietor:	Bernard F. Connolly
Address:	
City:	Petaluma, Ca.
Value:	$ _____
	John Burton Collection

CONNOLLY & BTO.

Location:	San Francisco
Face:	**CONNOLLY & BTO.**
	S.F.
Reverse:	**GEYSER SODA**
Bottom:	Blank
Rarity:	Rare
Date:	1862 - 1868
Proprietor:	Bernard & Michael Connolly
Address:	722 Front Street
City:	San Francisco
Value:	$ _____
	John Burton Collection

B. F. CONNOLLY

Location: Petaluma
Face: CONNOLLY & Bto.
              S.F.

Reverse: GEYSER SODA
Bottom: Dot
Rarity: Extremely Rare
Date: 1872 - 1873
Proprietor: Bernard F. Connolly
Address:
City: Petaluma, Ca.
Value: $ _____
John Burton Collection

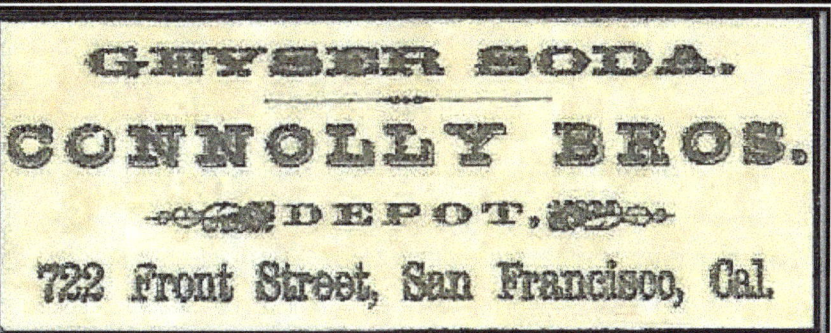

CROSS (Religious Bottle?)
Location:
Face: T (Cross)
Reverse: T (Cross)
Bottom: Iron Pontil mask
Rarity: Scarce
Date: 1850 – 1860's
Value: $ _____

Eastern blown bottle but most have been found in Georgetown, California.

CRYSTAL CIDER

Location:	San Francisco, Ca.
Face:	**CRYSTAL**
	S. W. CO.
	S.F.
	CIDER
Reverse:	Blank
Bottom:	Triangle
Rarity:	Extremely Rare
Date:	1885-1886
Proprietor:	Frank Maxsom & Sylvester Simmons
Address:	NE corner Stockton & Union Streets
City:	San Francisco, Ca.
Value:	$ _____

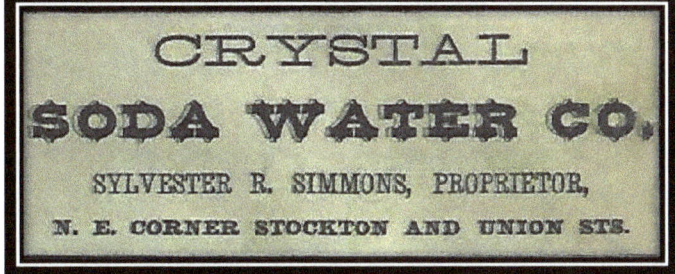

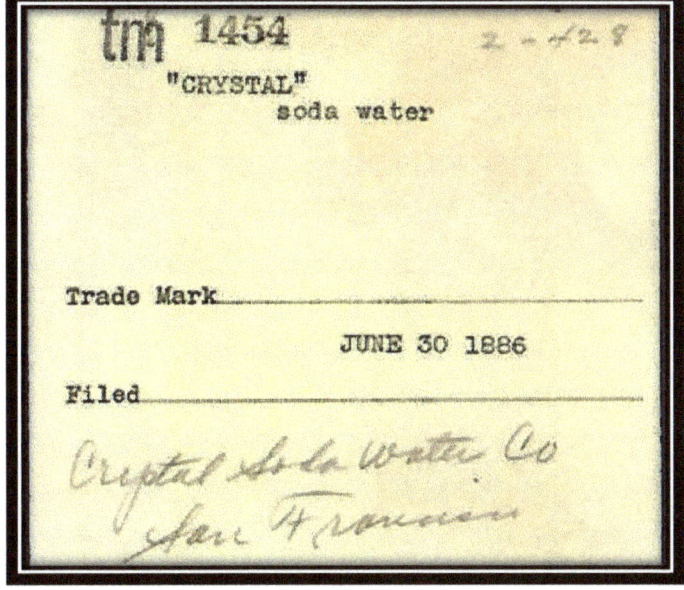

CRYSTAL SODA WATER

Location:	San Francisco
Face:	**CRYSTAL**
	SODA
	WATER CO.
Reverse:	**PATENTED**
	NOV. 12, 1872
	U.S.P.I.
Bottom:	Footed
Rarity:	Scarce in colors
Date:	1873 - 1874
	Frank Maxsom
	Sylvester Simons
	1875
	Frank Maxsom
	Sylvester Simons
	James Daly
	1876
	Frank Maxsom
	Sylvester Simons
	J. W. Roper
	W. H. Simons
	1877-1879
	Frank Maxsom
	Sylvester Simons
	J. W. Roper
	J. R. Roper
	W. H. Simons
	Jennie Simons
	1880-1889
	Frank Maxsom
	Sylvester Simon
	1873-1879
	NE corner Stockton & Union
	1888-1889
	2310 Mason Street
City:	San Francisco, Ca.
Value:	$ _____

With TAYLOR'S name on reverse
Collar Top

With TAYLOR'S name removed on reverse
Different Top

COLORIZATION KNOWN AS BENICIA GLASS

It is thought that a large tannery in Benicia allowed their waste water from the tanbark oak process that they used in curing hides to enter the bay unfiltered causing the effervescence. An average tannery of the day would process buckskins. cowhide, goat and sheep skins in the manufacturing of leather for gloves, shoes, jackets & other clothing material.

The toxic waste used to cure the hides flowed directly into the bay creating a chemical solution and reaction to the glass bottles. Fortunately, today the process has been improved and state laws now control the waste product.

John C. Burton Collection

A. W. Mc CUDWORTH (Formerly known as Chase & Co.)

Location:	San Francisco
Face:	**Mc CUDWORTH**
	& Co.
	SAN FRANCISCO
Reverse:	Blank
Bottom:	Iron Pontil Mark
Rarity:	Scarce
Date:	1856 - 1857
Proprietor:	A. W. Cudworth
Address:	Vallejo between Dupont & Kearney
	1858 - Cudworth & C0. (W.C. Pease)
	Excelsior Soda Factory
	Corner Hinckley & Pickney
	1859 – 1860 A. W. Cudworth
	Soda Manufactory, Vallejo between
	Dupont & Kearney
	1861 – Excelsior Soda Works
	Brader & Company
City:	San Francisco, Ca.
Value:	$ _____
	Rick Siri Collection

Additional examples of A. W. Cudworth Bottles
Bottle on left side without word Cal.

A.W. CUDWORTH/& Co./SAN FRANCISCO
Rick Siri Collection

A.W. CUDWORTH/& Co./SAN FRANCISCO/CAL.
Rick Siri Collection

W.E. DEAMER

Location:	Grass Valley
Face:	**DEAMER**
	GRASS VALLEY
Reverse:	**W. E. D.**
Bottom:	Blank
Rarity:	Scarce
Date:	1870's – 1880's
Proprietor:	William E. Deamer
Address:	School & Richardson Street
City:	Grass Valley, Ca.
Value:	$ _____

John C. Burton Collection

1854 - W. E. Deamer was in the soda business in Nevada City. Sold two months later and moved to Auburn then travelled to Europe.
1855 – He settled in Oroville.
1856 – Moved to Grass Valley and purchased the Snug Saloon.
1870 – Mid 1880's he manufactured ginger ale, cider and soda water located on the corner of School & Richardson Streets in Grass Valley.

DITZ & ELLERKAMP

Location:	San Francisco
Face:	**DITZ & ELLERKAMP**
	SAN FRANCISCO
	SODA WORKS
Reverse:	Blank
Bottom:	Blank
Date:	1868 – 1870
Rarity:	Extremely Rare
Proprietor:	Andrew Ditz, Benjamin Ellerkamp & Nickolas Gerdes
Address:	22 Hinckley near Dupont 1871-1872 Ellerkamp & Co. 22 Hinckley Street 1872-1873 Andrew Ditz Soda Bottler Ellerkamp now works as a driver for Bay City Soda Works 1873 John N. Gerdes proprietor of San Francisco Soda Works 22 Hinckley
City:	San Francisco, Ca.
Value:	$ _____

Eric McGuire Collection

DELAHANTY & SHELLY (Empire Soda Works)

Location:	San Francisco
Face:	D. S. & Co.
	SAN FRANCISCO
Reverse:	Blank
Bottom:	Blank
Rarity:	Aqua, Blue & Cobalt Very rare
	Apple Green Extremely Rare
Date:	1854-1855
:	John Delahanty & Michael Shelly
	83 Pine Street
	1856-1859
	John Delahanty & Michael Shelly
	Mission near Third Street
	1860-1863
	John Delahanty, Peter Shelly & Michael Fagen
	1864
	Delahanty, James & Lawarence McGuirk
	1865 Lawarnce McGuirk
City:	San Francisco, Ca.
Value:	$ _____

ADDITIONAL D. S. Co. SAN FRANCISCO BOTTLES

EAGLE SODA WORKS

Location:	Sacramento
Face:	Image of Eagle
Reverse:	Blank
Bottom:	Iron Pontil Mark
Rarity:	Open Pontil Very Rare
	Graphite Pontil Rare
Date:	1852 - 1863
Proprietor:	Owen Casey & James Kelly
Address:	107 K Street
City:	Sacramento
Value:	$ _____

Rick Siri Collection

This Eagle embossed bottle is attributed to Casey & Kelly prior to same embossed with C & K on the face of that bottle.

ADDITIONAL EAGLE BOTTLES

EASTERN CIDER CO.

Location:	San Francisco & Oakland
Face:	**EASTERN CIDER CO.**
Reverse:	Blank
Bottom:	Blank
Rarity:	Amber Scarce
	Olive & Apple Green Very Rare
ate:	1877 - 1882
Proprietor:	Donald Mitchell Superintendent
	719 Bryant Street, San Francisco
	OAKLAND
	1881-1882
	Mitchell, Blivens & Taylor
	13th & Franklin Street, Oakland
City:	San Francisco & Oakland, Ca.
Value:	$ _____
	John Burton Collection

ADDITIONAL EASTERN CIDER BOTTLES

EL-DORADO

Location:	Possibly Stockton
Face:	**EL-DORADO**
Reverse:	Blank
Bottom:	Blank
	Rarity: Semi Common
Date:	1860 – 1880 approximately
City:	Unknown
Value:	$ _____

John Burton Collection

EMPIRE SODA WORKS - D. S. & CO.

Location:	San Francisco
Face:	**EMPIRE SODA WORKS**
	D S & Co.
	SAN FRANCISCO
Reverse:	Blank
Bottom:	Blank
Rarity:	Aqua Rare, Blue & Green Very Rare
	Cobalt Extremely Rare
ate:	1861-1863 John Delahanty &
	Peter Skelly 29 Third Street
	1864-1865 Empire Soda Works D & M
	1866-1869 Fagan & Blevins & Co.
	NE Corner Third & Mission Streets
	1871 Empire Soda Works last year
	1880 Frank S. Waldo reinstated name
City:	San Francisco
Value:	$ _____

EMPIRE SODA WORKS – D. & M.

Location:	San Francisco
Face:	**EMPIRE SODA WORKS**
	D. & M.
	SAN FRANCISCO
Reverse:	Blank
Bottom:	Blank
Rarity:	Aqua, Blue & Green Rare
Date:	1864 - 1865
Proprietor:	John Delahanty, &
	Lawrence & James McGuirk
Address:	29 Third Street
City:	San Francisco, Ca.
Value:	$ _____

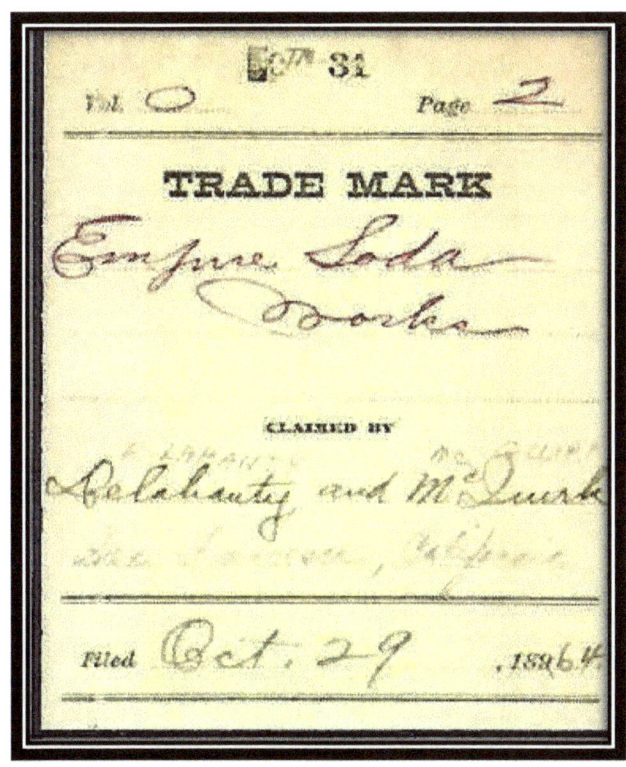

EMPIRE SODA WORKS – SAN FRANCISCO

Location:	San Francisco
Face:	**EMPIRE SODA WORKS**
	SAN FRANCISCO
Reverse:	Blank
Bottom:	Blank
Rarity:	Aqua Common
	Colors Rare
Date:	1861 - 1870
	Michael Fagen & James Blivens
Address:	NE corner Third & Harrison
	1870-1871
	Fagan, Blivens, & Henry Price
	353 Third Street
City:	San Francisco, Ca.
Value:	$ _____

ADDITIONAL EMPIRE SODA WORKS COLORS

EMPIRE SODA WORKS – SAN FRANCISCO & ALAMEDA

Location:	San Francisco & Alameda
Face:	FRANK
	S
	WALDO
Reverse:	Blank
Bottom:	Blank

SAN FRANCISCO

Rarity:	Rare
Date:	1880 - 1881
	Frank S. Waldo
Address:	1717 Market Street
City:	San Francisco, Ca.

ALAMEDA

	1881-1882
Address:	N Eagle Avenue between Oak & Park Alameda, Ca.
Value:	$ _____

EMPIRE SODA WORKS - VALLEJO

Location:	Vallejo
Face:	**EMPIRE**
	SODA
	WORKS
Reverse:	**VALLEJO**
	E. McG
Bottom:	Blank
Rarity:	Extremely Rare
Date:	1867-1874
Proprietor:	Edward McGettigan
Address:	Corner Florida & Sonoma
City:	Vallejo, Ca.
Value:	$ _____

McGettigan purchased the soda operation of James McGarvey at the corner oy Carolina & Marin Streets in 1874. At this time, he started the Pioneer Brewery that operated until approximately 1880.

EAGLE - EMPIRE SODA WORKS - VALLEJO

Location:	Vallejo
Face:	**EMPIRE SODA WORKS**
	(Branches)
	VALLEJO
Reverse:	Image of Eagle
Bottom:	Blank
Rarity:	Rare
Date:	1874-1878
Proprietor:	Frank & Charles O'Grady
Address:	Corner Sonoma & Carolina 1878-1880's relocated to the Corner of Sonoma & Florida. F. McDermott became a partner for a short time in the early 1880's only Charles O'Grady operated the soda factory until the early 1890's.
City:	Vallejo, Ca.
Value:	$ _____

John C. Burton Collection

EAGLE - EMPIRE SODA WORKS - VALLEJO

THE EXCELSIOR WATER – SAN FRANCISCO

Location:	San Francisco
Panels: (Vertical)	**THE EXCELSIOR WATER**
Reverse:	Blank
Bottom:	Blank
Rarity:	Aqua & Apple Green Scarce
	Emeral Green Rare
Date:	1856-1857
Proprietor:	Hedley & Company
Address:	157 California Street
	1858-1859
	A. W. Cudworth, & W.c. Pease
	1860-1861
	A. W. Cudworth
	Vallejo Street between Dupont & Kearny
City:	San Francisco, Ca.
Value:	$ _____

EXCELSIOR SODA & MINERAL WATER – LOS ANGELES

Location:	Los Angeles
Face:	**EXCELSIOR**
	SODA
	&
	MINERAL
	WATER
	FACRTORY
Reverse:	Blank
Bottom:	Blank
Rarity:	Aqua & Lime Green Rare
Date:	1875
Proprietor:	Fritz & Aocherblum
Address:	Round House Main Street
City:	Los Angeles, Ca.
Value:	$ _____

J. A. FARRELL
Location: Grass Valley
Face: J. A. FARRELL
             GRASS VALLEY

Reverse: F
Bottom: Blank
Rarity: Aqua & Light Green Common
Date: 1860's
Proprietor: J. A. Farrell
Address: Mill Street
City: Grass Valley, Ca.
Value: $ _____
             John C. Burton Collection

F. M. MODESTO

Location:	Modesto
Face:	F. M. MODESTO
Reverse:	Blank
Bottom:	Blank
Rarity:	Scarce
Date:	1875 - 1880
Proprietor:	Frederick Meinecke
Address:	Ninth Street
City:	Modesto, Ca.
Value:	$ _____

John C. Burton Collection

D. L. FONSECA & COMPANY
Location: San Francisco
Face: **D. L. FONSECA & CO.**

Reverse: **JAMAICA**
                 CHAMPAGNE
                   BEER
                     S.F.

Bottom: Blank
Rarity: Very Rare
Date: 1871
Proprietor: David L. Fonseca
Address;   17 Ellis Street
City: San Francisco, Ca.
Value: $ _____

David L. Fonseca was a physician who moved nine times from Oakland to San Francisco twice.

Starting in 1871 he sold Jamaica Champagne Beer out of Schord's Saloon located at 531 California Street in San Francisco.

1885-1886 he was a manufacturer of Triumph Bitters at 17 Ellis Street in San Francisco.

1887 Listed as a physician changing his name to D. L. Fonseca.

1879 he is listed as a collector for the "Odorless Excavation Apparatus Co." cleaning out cisterns and outhouses.

JAMAICA CHAMPAGNE BEER

JAMAICA CHAMPAGNE BEER.

THE GREAT

Temperance and Summer Drink!

COOLING, REFRESHING AND RESTORING,

Antespeptic, Anti-Spasmodic, and Healthy.

THE BEST DRINK Early in the Morning, being a powerful Anti-spasmodic.

THE BEST DRINK in the Heat of the Day, being cooling and refreshing; therefore well suited to those suffering from the effects of heat, and as a restorative to those suffering from over exertion or exhaustion of mind and body, being also well suited to remove the ill effects of spirituous drinks.

THE BEST DRINK at Sea, being a powerful Antespeptic and gentle laxative.

THE BEST DRINK for all who require a beverage at once harmless, agreeable, effervescing and sparkling, producing a delightful foam, giving tone to the stomach and imparting a delightful glowth to the whole system, and containing no poisonous gases.

Let all try our manufacture, and universal judgment will pronounce it the best and most agreeable drink in the market.

Orders left at L. G. SCHORD'S, 531 California street as well as at the manufactory, **641 THIRD STREET**, will receive prompt and immediate attention.

ap11-2p2w   **D. L. FONSECA & CO.**

FOUNTAIN & TALLMAN

Location:	Sacramento
Face:	**FOUNTAIN & TALLMAN**
	CALFA.
Reverse:	**BRIDGETON**
	N. J.
Bottom:	Iron Pontil Mark
Rarity:	Extremely Rare
Date:	1850 – 1860 approximately
Proprietor:	W. F. Fountain & Tallman
Address:	?
City:	Sacramento, Ca.
Value:	$ _____

G. & G. MERCED

Location:	Merced
Face:	G. & G. MERCED
Reverse:	Blank
Bottom:	Blank
Rarity:	Rare
Date:	1874-1881
Proprietor:	Giovanni Galliano
Address:	Merced Soda Works
City:	Merced, Ca.
Value	$ _____

1882 he became partner with Frank Borello in Fresno Until 1893 where they operated the Fresno Soda Works. In 1893, Galliano moved back to Merced employed as a grocer.

J.N. GERDES

Location:	San Francisco
Panels: (Vertical)	J. N. GERDES S. F.
Reverse:	MINERAL WATER
Bottom:	Blank
Rarity:	Aqua Scarce Green & Blue Rare
Date:	1873 - 1877
Proprietor:	John N. Gerdes
Address:	22 Hinckley Street 733 Union Street
City:	San Francisco, Ca.
Value:	$ _____
	John C. Burton Collection

1860's Gerdes was listed as a driver for the California Soda Works.

1873-1875 proprietor of San Francisco Soda Works 22 Hinckley Street moving to 733 Union Street From 1876 to 1877.

1877-1880 Henry Gerdes & William Bruning purchased thr company and Bruning bought out Gerdes in 1880.

ADDITIONAL GERDES MINERAL WATER BOTTLES

GEYSER SODA

Location:	San Francisco
ace:	**GEYSER SODA**
Reverse:	**NATURAL MINERAL WATER FROM LITTON SPRINGS SONOMA CO. CAL.**
Bottom:	Blank
Rarity:	Semi Common
Date:	1886 - B. M. Hungerford manager
	1887- William S. Moore manager
	1888- George E. Madison manager
	1889-1893 Louis Lowe Jr. manager
Location:	152 New Montgomery Street
City:	San Francisco, Ca.
Value:	$ _____
	John C. Burton Collection

Litton (Lytton) Springs located 4 miles north of Healdsburg in Sonoma County.

GEYSER SODA SPRINGS

Location:	San Francisco
Face:	GEYSER
	SODA
	SPRINGS
Reverse:	NATURAL
	MINERAL WATER
Bottom:	Blank
Rarity:	Common
Date:	1891 - 1898
Proprietor:	E. L. Lowe
Address:	1891-1892 - 152 Montgomery Street
	1893-1894 – 29 Stuart Street
	1895-1896 – R. H. Curry manager
	41 Stevenson Street
	1896-1897 – R. M. Horton manager
	43 Stevenson Street
City:	San Francisco, Ca.
Value:	$ _____
	John C. Burton Collection

GEYSER

Location:	San Francisco
Face:	GEYSER
	NATURAL BOILED
	MINERAL WATER
Reverse:	Blank
Bottom:	Blank
Rarity:	Dime a dozen
Date:	1897 - 1898
Manager:	R. M. Horton manager
Address:	43 Stevenson Street
City:	San Francisco, Ca.
Value:	$ _____
	John C. Burton Collection

GHIRADELLI - OAKLAND

Location:	Oakland
Face:	**GHIRADELLI**
	BRANCH
	OAKLAND
Reverse:	Blank
Bottom:	Blank
Rarity:	Blue & Cobalt Rare
	Green Extremely Rare
Date:	1863 - 1869
Proprietor:	Domenico Ghiradelli
Address:	Third & Broadway
City:	Oakland, Ca.
Value:	$ _____
	John C. Burton Collection

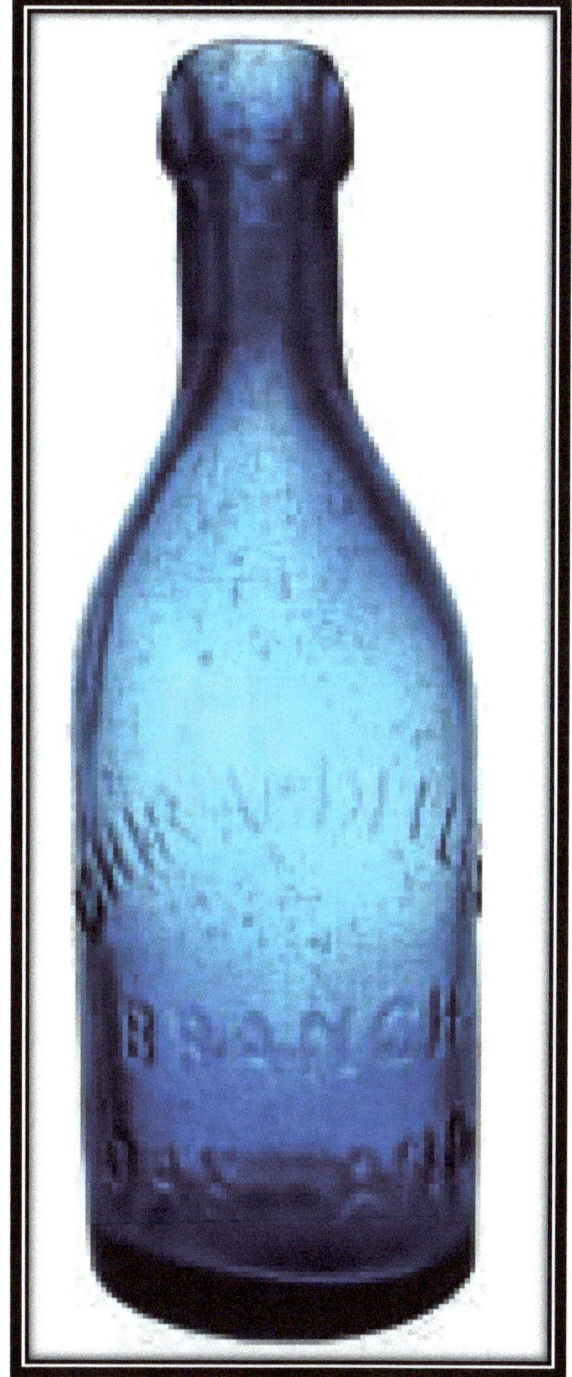

1850 Domenico Ghiradelli was a grocer in San Francisco on Battery Street between Broadway & Vallejo.

1852 Ghiradelli & Cox, confection business, located at 194 Washington Street.

1853 Domenico opened a branch in Oakland Corner Third & Broadway.

1854, Mrs. Ghiradelli was the proprietor of the business selling syrups, liquor, coffee and soda water.

1863-1869, in Oakland, he was listed as Importer, wholesaler, & retail dealer in Groceries, foreign wines, & liquors, plus English, French, Japan & East India goods and operating a soda water factory.

1879, he moved to corner of Broadway & 7th Streets adding hardware & crockery.

GHIRADELLI & CO.

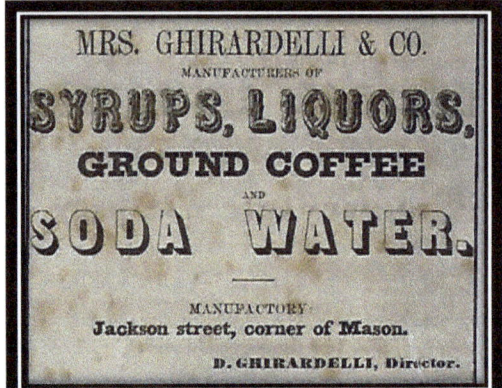

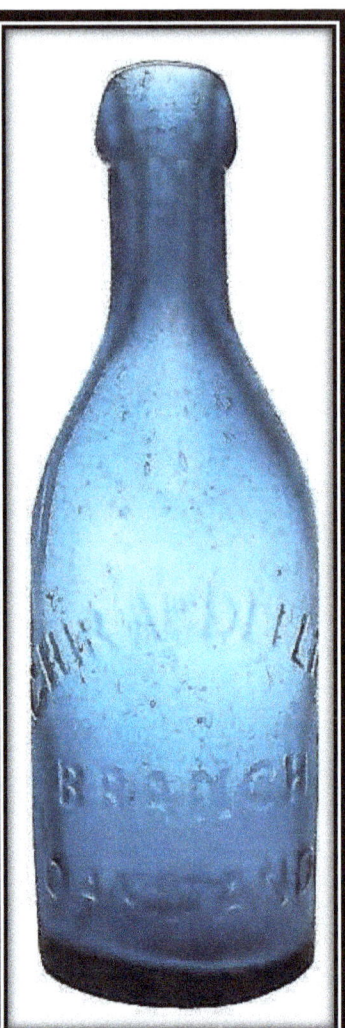

GOLDEN GATE

Location:	San Francisco
Face:	GOLDEN GATE
Reverse:	Blank
Bottom:	Iron Pontil Mark
Rarity:	Aqua: Scarce
	Green: Rare
	Blue: Very Rare
	Cobalt: Extremely Rare
	Amber: Off the Charts
Date:	1850's – 1860's approximate
Proprietor:	James Cartwright
Address:	Yankee Jim's Saloon?
City:	Forest Hill in Placerville
Value:	$ _____

Rick Siri Collection

Majority of Golden Gate bottles were dug in Forest Hill, Placer County, under a saloon known as Yankee Jim's.

James Cartwright arrived in 1850 opening a supply store. In 1852 he was proprietor of a billiard and bowling (ten pins) parlor in what was known as the Golden Gate saloon.

In 1853 the Golden Gate Saloon was owned by Cartwright & Pellygrove and became the center piece of the area for political assemblies.

The Golden Gate Saloon fell to fire in 1862.

ADDITIONAL GOLDEN GATE COLORS

GOLDEN WEST – NAPA COUNTY

Location:	San Francisco
Face:	**GOLDEN WEST**
	NAPA
	COUNTY
	SODA SPRINGS
Reverse:	**NATURAL**
	MINERAL WATER
	NAPA
	COUNTY, CAL.
Bottom:	Blank
Rarity:	Rare
Date:	1895 - 1897
Proprietor:	Eugene Herve & Pierre Somps
Address:	622 Laguna Street
City:	San Francisco, Ca.
Value:	$ _____
	Mike Southworth Collection

GOLDEN WEST – NAPA COUNTY

Location:	San Francisco
Face:	**GOLDEN WEST**
	NAPA
	COUNTY
	NAT'L SPRINGS
Reverse:	**NATURAL**
	MINERAL WATER
	FROM THE
	GOLDEN WEST SPRINGS
	NAPA
	COUNTY, CAL.
Bottom:	Blank
	Rarity: Extremely Rare Variation
Date:	1895 - 1897
Proprietor:	Eugene Herve & Pierre Somps
Address:	622 Laguna Street
City:	San Francisco, Ca.
Value:	$ _____
	Mike Southworth Collection

GOLDEN WEST – NAPA COUNTY

Location:	San Francisco
Face:	**GOLDEN WEST**
	NAPA
	SODA SPRINGS
Reverse:	**NATURAL**
	MINERAL WATER
	NAPA
	COUNTY, CAL.
Bottom:	Blank
Rarity:	Rare
Date:	1895 - 1897
Proprietor:	Eugene Herve & Pierre Somps
Address:	622 Laguna Street
City:	San Francisco, Ca.
Value:	$ _____
	Mike Southworth Collection

HERVE & SOMPS

Location:	San Francisco
Face:	E. HERVE & P. SOMPS
	PROPS.
	622 LAGUNA ST.
	S. F. CAL.
Reverse:	NATURAL
	MINERAL WATER
	FROM THE
	GOLDEN WEST SPRINGS
	NAPA
	COUNTY, CAL.
Bottom:	Blank
Rarity:	Rare
	Bottle next page Scarce
Date:	1895-1896
Proprietor:	Eugene Herve & Pierre Somps
Address:	622 Laguna Street
	1896-1897 Golden West Springs
	Herve & Somps 622 Laguna St.
City:	San Francisco, Ca.
Value:	$ _____

HERVE & SOMPS

1895, Eugene Herve & Pierre Somps started the Golden West Springs Co., however, there was never a Golden West Springs in Napa County. They bottled their water at Walter's Spring's in Napa bottling under the name of Natural Mineral Water from Golden West Springs, Napa County.

The mold of this bottle is from J. Somps & J. Meillette who bottled from 1892-1895. The same bottle was used by F. Paillet from 1901 to 1906. Earthquake.

John C. Burton Collection

EDWARD HIGGINS

Location:	Oroville
Face:	E. HIGGINS
	OROVILLE
Reverse:	Blank
Bottom:	Blank
Rarity:	Rare
Date:	1875 - 1887
Proprietor:	Edward Higgins
Address:	Montgomery Street
City:	Oroville, Ca.
Value:	$ _____

HOGAN & THOMPSON

Location:	San Francisco
Face:	**HOGAN & THOMPSON**
	SAN FRANCISCO
	CAL.
Reverse:	**UNION GLASS WORKS**
	PHILADELPHIA
Bottom:	Iron Pontil Mark
Rarity:	Extremely Rare all colors
Date:	1850's
Proprietor:	P. J. Hogan & George C. Thompson
Address:	Union Street near Stockton
City:	San Francisco, Ca.
Value:	$ _____

HOGAN & THOMPSON

1854 - P. J. Hogan Union Soda Factory, Union Place
   H. Hogan, Union Soda Factory, Union Place
   George Thompson, Union Soda Factory, Union Place
1856 – George Thompson & J. McEwin manufacturing soda north side of Union St.

HOLLISTER SODA WORKS

Location:	Hollister
Face:	HOLLISTER
	SODA
	WORKS
	A. MANS
Reverse:	Blank
Bottom:	Blank
Rarity:	Scarce in Aqua
	Extremely Rare in Blue
Date:	Late 1870's
Proprietor:	Alfred Mans
Address:	Fifth Street
City:	Hollister, Ca.
Value:	$ _____

Alfred Mans was proprietor of the French Hotel & Restaurant in Hollister in the 1870's.

In 1880's it was listed as the French Saloon & Restaurant located on Fifth Street in Hollister.

At the same time, he was selling liquor and soda water probably from the same address.

HUMBOLDT

Location:	Eureka
Face:	**HUMBOLDT**
	ARTESIAN
	MINERAL WATER
Reverse:	**EUREKA**
	(Vertical)
Bottom:	Blank
Date:	1893 – 1897
Rarity:	Scarce
Proprietor:	J. Monroe manager
Address:	Mile south of Eureka
City:	Eureka, Ca.
Value:	$ _____

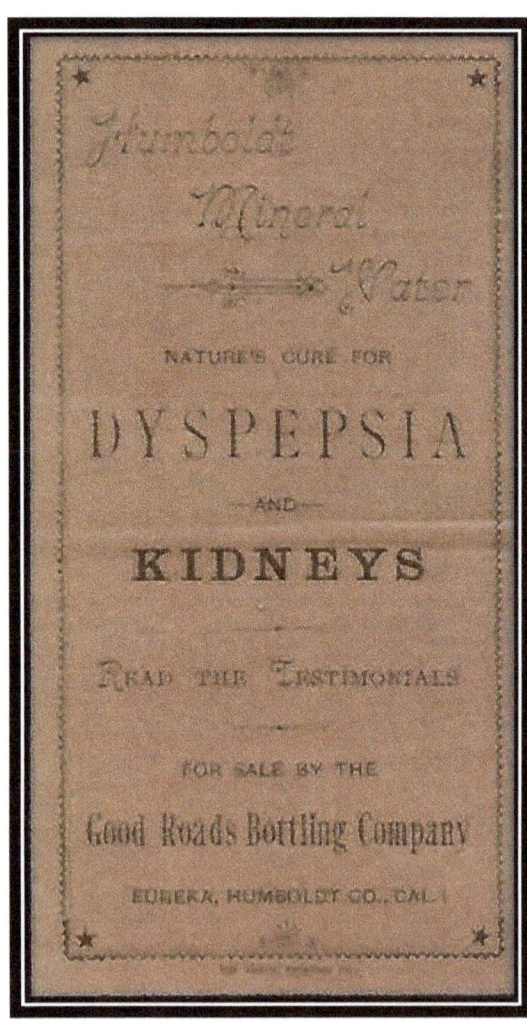

HUMBOLDT ARTESIAN MINERAL WATER
John C. Burton Collection

ITALIAN SODA WATER

Location:	San Francisco
Face:	**ITALIAN**
	SODA WATER
	MANUFACTORY
	SAN FRANCISCO
Reverse:	**UNION GLASS WORKS**
	PHIL A
Bottom:	Iron Pontil Mark
Date:	1856 – 1863
Rarity:	All Colors Scarce
Proprietor:	1856-1857 Joseph Spinoni
	SW corner Powell & Filbert
	1858-1860 Stevenson near Anne St.
	Between 2nd & 3rd.
	1860-1862 - S. Grellier & Co.
	Italian Soda Works 192 Stevenson
City:	San Francisco, Ca.
Value:	$ _____

There is a variant misspelled "WOKS"
Variant is a blank reverse

In 1865, James McEwen was listed as the owner of the California Soda Works located at 192 Stevenson Street.

ADDITIONAL ITALIAN SODA WORKS BOTTLE COLORS

ITALIAN/SODA WATER/MANUFACTURY/SAN FRANCISCO
UNION GLASS WORKS/PHILA.
Rick Siri Collection

JACKSON'S NAPA SODA SPRINGS

Location:	San Francisco
Face:	JACKSON'S
	NAPA
	SODA
	SPRING'S
Reverse:	NATURAL
	MINERAL WATER
Bottom:	Blank
Rarity:	Aqua: Common
	Shades of Blue: Scarce
	Shades of Green: Rare
Date:	1873 - 1885
Proprietor:	Col. John P. Jackson
Address:	50 miles north of San Francisco
City:	San Francisco, Ca.
Value:	$ _____

JACKSON'S NAPA SODA SPRINGS
NATURAL MINERAL WATER

JACKSON'S NAPA SODA SPRINGS (Tall Bottle)

Location: San Francisco
Face: JACKSON'S
                 NAPA
                 SODA
                 SPRING'S

Reverse: NATURAL
              MINERAL WATER
               THIS BOTTLE
               IS NEVER SOLD

Bottom: Blank
Rarity: Semi Common
Date: 1885 - 1895
Proprietor: Col. John P. Jackson
Address: North of San Francisco
City: San Francisco, Ca.
Value: $ _____
              John C. Burton Collection

123

JACKSON'S NAPA SODA SPRING'S

Location: Napa
Face: JACKSON'S
NAPA
SODA
SPRING'S

Reverse: NATURAL
MINERAL WATER
THIS BOTTLE
NEVER SOLD

Bottom: Blank
Rarity: Semi Common
Year 1873 – 1900
Proprietor: John P. Jackson
Address: North of San Francisco
City: San Francisco, Ca.
Value $ _____

John C. Burton Collection
Lighter Richard Siri Collection

JACKSON'S NAPA SODA

Location:	San Francisco
Face:	JACKSON'S
	NAPA
	SODA
Reverse:	A
	NATURAL
	MINERAL WATER
	JACKSON'S
	THIS BOTTLE
	IS NEVER SOLD
Bottom:	Blank
Rarity:	Dime a dozen
Date:	1895 – 1906
Proprietor:	Col. John P. Jackson
Address:	North of San Francisco
City:	San Francisco, Ca.
Value:	$ _____
	John C. Burton Collection

JACKSON'S NAPA SODA SPRINGS

Location:	San Francisco
Face:	JACKSON'S
	NAPA
	SODA
	SPRING'S
Reverse:	NATURAL
	MINERAL WATER
Bottom:	B. & CO.
Rarity:	Rare
Date:	1886 – 1887
Proprietor:	William A. Brown Agent
Address:	North of San Francisco
City:	San Francisco, Ca.
Value:	$ _____
	John C. Burton Collection

Two different lettering on bottom

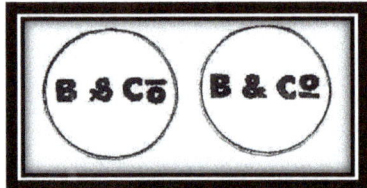

JACKSON'S NAPA SODA SPRINGS

Location:	Petaluma
Face:	JACKSON'S
	NAPA
	SODA
	SPRING'S
Reverse:	NATURAL
	MINERAL WATER
	B. F. CONNOLLY
Bottom:	Blank
Rarity:	Rare
Date:	1873 - 1885
Proprietor:	Bernard F. Connolly
Address:	
City:	Petaluma, Ca.
Value:	$ _____
	John C. Burton Collection

JACKSON'S NAPA SODA SPRINGS

Location:	San Francisco
Face:	JACKSON'S
	NAPA
	SODA
	SPRING'S
Reverse:	NATURAL
	MINERAL WATER
Bottom:	C. & P.
Rarity:	Rare
Date:	1882 – 1883
Proprietor:	Cutler & Pearson
Address:	
City:	San Francisco, Ca.
Value:	$ _____
	John C. Burton collection

Cutler & Pearson

128

JACKSON'S NAPA SODA SPRINGS

Location:	San Francisco
Face:	JACKSON'S
	NAPA
	SODA
	SPRING'S
Reverse:	NATURAL
	MINERAL WATER
	M. SILVA
Bottom:	Blank
Rarity:	Scarce
Date:	1878 – 1890
Proprietor:	Manuel Silva
Address:	87 Main Street Corner
	Main & Start Street
City:	San Francisco, Ca.
Value:	$ _____

John C. Burton Collection

JACKSON'S NAPA SODA SPRINGS

Location:	Napa
Face:	JACKSON'S
	NAPA
	SODA
	SPRING'S
Reverse:	NATURAL
	MINERAL WATER
	ED HENRY
Bottom:	Blank
Rarity:	Rare
Date:	1901 - 1906
Proprietor:	Ed Henry
Address:	
City:	Napa, Ca.
Value:	$ _____

John C. Burton Collection

JACKSON'S NAPA SODA SPRINGS

Location:	Vallejo
Face:	JACKSON'S
	NAPA
	SODA
	SPRING'S
Reverse:	NATURAL
	MINERAL WATER
	F. M.
	VALLEJO
Bottom:	Blank
Rarity:	Extremely Rare
Date:	1873 - 1885
Proprietor:	Fred Michaelis
Address:	
City:	Vallejo, Ca.
Value:	$ _____

JACKSON'S NAPA SODA SPRINGS

Location:	Pasadena (Southern California)
Face:	JACKSON'S
	NAPA
	SODA
	SPRING'S
Reverse:	NATURAL
	MINERAL WATER
	S. P. & CO.
Bottom:	S. & P.
Rarity:	Rare
Date:	1873 - 1885
Proprietor:	M. A. Sattley & A. J. Page Agents for Jackson's Napa Soda in Southern California
Address:	?
City:	Pasadena, Ca.

JACKSON'S NAPA SODA SPRINGS

Location:	Fairfax, Ca.
Face:	JACKSON'S
	NAPA
	SODA
	SPRING'S
Reverse:	NATURAL
	MINERAL WATER
	A. BRESSON
Bottom:	Blank
Rarity:	Extremely Rare
Date:	1873 – 1885
Proprietor:	A. Bresson agent for Jackson's Napa Soda in Marin County
Address:	?
City:	Fairfax – San Rafael Area

JACKSON'S NAPA SODA

Location:	San Francisco
Face:	JACKSON'S NAPA SODA S. F.
Reverse:	Blank
Bottom:	527
Date:	1873 – 1900
Rarity:	Scarce
Proprietor:	John P. Jackson
Address:	North of San Francisco
City:	San Francisco, Ca.
Value:	$ _____

John C. Burton Collection
Lighter Richard Siri Collection

KIMBALL & Co.

Location:	Marysville
Face:	**KIMBALL & CO.**
Reverse:	Blank
Bottom:	Iron Pontil Mark
Rarity:	Scarce
Date:	1853 - 1856
Proprietor:	Charles H. Kimball
Address:	Corner B & Fourth Street
	1856 Listed at B Street between
	First & Front Streets
City:	Marysville, Ca.
Value:	$ _____

Charles Kimball located a soda water business in 1853 in Marysville. The soda water company was located on corner of B and Front Streets until 1855 when he moved to corner Front & First Street in 1856.

He sold the business in September 1856.

LODTMANN, E & JL

Location:	Knights Ferry, Ca.
Face:	R & JL
Reverse:	Blank
Bottom:	Blank
Rarity:	Extremely Rare
Date:	1867-1874
Proprietor:	E. & J. Lodtmann
Address:	Knights Ferry General Store

1880's the brothers moved to Santa Cruz bottling water there. They retired and went into real estate.

City:	Santa Cruz, Ca.
Value:	$ _____

B. R. LIPPINCOTT

Location:	Stockton
Face:	B. R. LIPPINCOTT
	STOCKTON
Reverse:	SUPERIOR MINERAL WATER
	UNION GLASS WORKS
Bottom:	Iron Pontil Mask
Rarity:	Rare with Iron Pontil
	Extremely Rare with open Pontil
Date:	1852
Proprietor:	B.R. Lippincott
Address:	Corner Weber & San Joaquin Streets
City:	Stockton, Ca.
Value:	$ _____

LIPPINCOTT & VAUGHN

Location:	Stockton
Face:	L. & V.
Reverse:	Blank
Bottom:	Iron Pontil Mask
Date:	1852 – 1857
Rarity:	Aqua & Green Rare
Proprietor:	B.R. Lippincott & A. F. Vaughn
Address:	Corner Weber & San Joaquin Streets
City:	Stockton, Ca.
Value:	$ _____

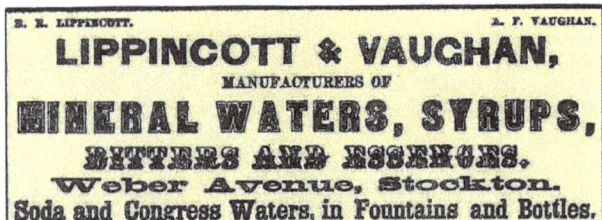

L & B – LIPPINCOTT & BELDING

Location:	Stockton & Marysville
Face:	L. & B.
Reverse:	Blank
Bottom:	Iron Pontil Mask
Variant:	B slugged over V
Date:	1857 – 1870
Rarity:	Very Rare
Proprietor:	1857–1870 Lippincott & Belding
Address:	Corner Weber & San Joaquin Streets
City:	Stockton
	1863-1870 Lippincott & Belding Corner 2nd & Virgin Alley
City:	Marysville
Value:	$ _____

LITTONS MINERAL WATER

Location:	Healdsburg
Face:	LITTON'S MINERAL WATER
Reverse:	HEALDSBURG (Vertical)
Bottom:	LITTON'S MINERAL WATER
Rarity:	Extremely Rare Pint Size Bottle
Year(s)	1870's
Proprietor:	Litton (Lytton)
Address:	
City:	Litton Springs
Value:	$ _____

Frank Ritz Collection

LYTTON

Location:	Lytton Springs
Face:	LYTTON
	GEYSER
	SODA
	SPRINGS
Reverse:	NATURAL
	MINERAL WATER
Bottom:	Blank
Rarity:	Semi Common
Date:	1894 - 1999
Proprietor:	Phillip Kyle manager
Address:	41 Second Street
City:	San Francisco, Ca.
Value:	$ _____
	John Burton Collection

LOS ANGELES SODA MINERAL WATER FACTORY

Location:	Los Angeles
Face:	**LOS ANGELES SODA & MINERAL WATER FACTORY**
Reverse:	**H. W. STOLL**
Bottom:	Blank
Rarity:	Rare
Date:	1875 – 1874
	Henry W. Stoll & W. H. Huber
	1875- 1884
	Henry W. Stoll - 13 Aliso Street
	1878-1884
	Henry Stoll - 38 Saivain Street
	1884-1900
	Henry Stoll & P. C. Stoll
	107 Sansevain Street
City:	Los Angeles, Ca.
Value:	$ _____

Henry & P. C. Stoll were also listed as owners of Pasadena Soda Works at 219 South Fair Oaks Avenue in the late 1880's.

LOS ANGELES SODA WATER WORKS,
H. W. STOLL & CO., Proprietors.
Manufacturers of
Soda Water, Sarsaparilla, Ginger Ale, Mineral Waters, Champagne Cider, and all kinds of Syrups.
No. 107 SAINSEVIAN STREET.
All orders promptly attended to.   Trade ★ Mark.   Telephone No. 103.

LOS ANGELES SODA WORKS (LOS ANGELES MISSPELT)

Location:	Los Angeles
Face:	H. W. STOLL
	LOS ANGELOS
	SODA WORKS
Reverse:	Blank
Bottom:	Blank
Rarity:	Extremely Rare
Date:	Henry W. Stoll - 13 Aliso Street
	1878-1884
	Henry Stoll - 38 Saivain Street
	1884-1900
City:	Los Angeles, Ca.
Value:	$ _____
	Dr. Tom Jacobs Collection

☞ **CERTIFICATE OF PARTNERSHIP** of the firm of H. W. Stoll & Co., doing business in the city of Los Angeles, county of Los Angeles, State of California.

We, the undersigned persons, hereby certify that the above described partnership is composed of the following persons and no others, whose names and places of residence are as follows, to-wit:

H. W. STOLL, Los Angeles.
FR. AOCKERBLUM, Los Angeles.

In witness whereof we have hereunto affixed our hands and seals this 10th day of August, 1875.

HENRY W. STOLL,
FR. AOCKERBLUM.

STATE OF CALIFORNIA, } ss.
County of Los Angeles. }

On this ninth day of September, in the year 1875, before me, J. J. Warner, a Notary Public, personally appeared Henry W. Stoll and Fr. Aockerblum, both residents of the State and county aforesaid, and known to me to be the persons whose names are subscribed to the within instrument, and they severally acknowledged to me that they executed the same.

Witness my hand and official seal this ninth day of September, 1875. J. J. WARNER.
Notary Public.

LYNDE & PUTNAM

Location:	San Francisco
Face:	LYNDE & PUTNAM MINERAL WATERS SAN FRANCISCO CAL.A
Reverse:	UNION GLASS WORKS PHILAD
Bottom:	Iron Pontil Mark
Rarity:	Extremely Rare
Variant:	Without Slug Plate
Date:	1850 - 1851
Proprietor:	J. D. Lynde & H. W. Putnam
Address:	Between Washington & Jackson Moved to Sansome Street
City:	San Francisco, Ca.
Value:	$ _____

February 18, 1852 F. C. Chase placed an advertisement that he purchased Lynde & Putnam Mineral Water Company

ADDITIONAL LYNDE & PUTNAM BOTTLES
NOTICE THE DIFFERENCE OF THE DARK BLUE BOTTLES TOP

M
Location: Stockton
Face: M
Reverse: Blank
Bottom: Blank
Date: Late 1870's early 1880's
Rarity: Extremely Rare
Proprietor: E. May & Co.
Address:
City: Stockton, Cal.
Value: $ _____

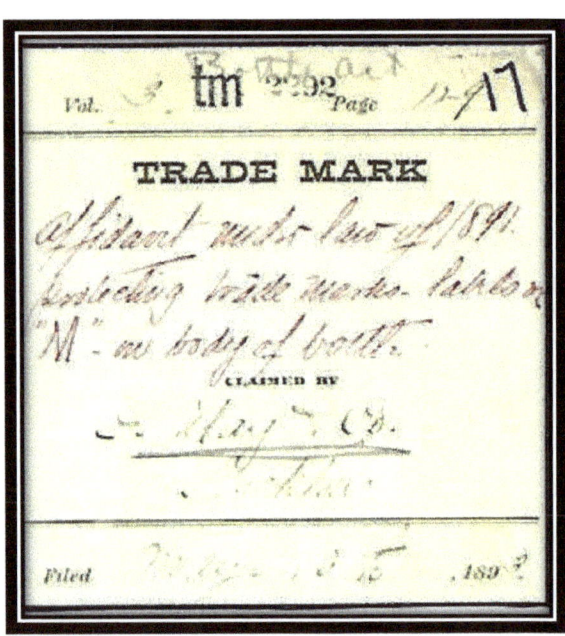

E. May bottled both soda waters and cider.

MARTINELLI SODA WORKS

Location:	Watsonville
Face:	MARTINELLI SODA WORKS M. S.
Reverse:	Blank
Bottom:	Blank
Date:	1875 - 1890
Rarity:	Semi Common
Proprietor:	Stephen Martinelli
Address:	
City:	Watsonville, Ca
Value:	$ _____
	John C. Burton Collection

Martinelli sold hard cider in 1868 expanding to soda and mineral waters.

Mc EWIN

Location:	San Francisco
Panels:	Mc EWIN
Reverse:	SAN FRANCISCO
Bottom:	Blank
Date:	1863 – 1870
Rarity:	Scarce
	One Amethyst known
Proprietor:	James Mc Ewin
Address:	190 – 192 Stevenson Street
City:	San Francisco, Ca.
Value:	$ _____
	Eric McGuire Collection

McEwen started in 1856 in partnership with George Thompson co-owner of Union Mineral Water Works.

In 1862 he had a delivery wagon business and in 1863-1864 he was proprietor of California Soda Works, 192 Stevenson Street moving to 194 Stevenson Street in 1867-1869 then to 190 Stevenson Street from 1869 to 1870.
   (Street numbers may have changed)
In 1871 he became proprietor of Bay City Soda Water Co.

TO SODA MANUFACTURERS
AND
All Others Dealing in Bottles.

YOU ARE HEREBY CAUTIONED against filling, using, dealing with or trafficking in any bottles of the following make or description:
   My bottles are of the ordinary sized Soda Bottle, each of which is pentagonal, or ten-sided, on one of which sides is blown in raised letters "McEWIN," and on the opposite, or reverse side, "SAN FRANCISCO."
   All are hereby informed that on the 23d day of May last I filed in the office of the Secretary of State, of California, a description and drawings of the above described bottles, and the words thereon as aforesaid, claiming the same as my Trade Mark.
   Any person hereafter found using, claiming, or dealing with any bottle of the above description, will be prosecuted to the full extent of the law.
JAMES McEWEN.
San Francisco, June 1st, 1867.   jy16-1w*

McGEE, B. J.
Location: Benicia
Face: B. J. McGEE
BENICIA
Reverse: Blank
Bottom: Blank
Date: 1867
Rarity: Common
Proprietor: B. J. McGee
Address: H & First Street
City: Benicia, Ca.
Value $ _____
John C. Burton Collection

Barney McGee was an attorney and bottled a short time in Benicia relocating to San Francisco.

His former Benicia location became the site of John Rurger's Benicia Brewery.

McGEE, B. J.
Location: San Francisco
Face: **B. J. McGEE**
SAN FRANCISCO
Reverse: Blank
Bottom: Blank
Rarity: Extremely Rare
Color: Aqua & Green
Date: 1869 – 1873

Proprietor: B. J. McGee
Union Soda Works
Address: 107 Fifth Street
City: San Francisco, Ca.
Value: $ _____

Although the B. J. McGee is common, the B. J. McGee San Franciscsi is extremely rare.

MERRIAM'S

Location:	Sonora, Cal.
Face:	MERRIAM'S
Reverse:	Blank
Bottom:	Blank
Rarity:	Extremely Rare
Color:	Cobalt
Date:	1852-1856
Proprietor:	J. Merriam & J.L. Merriam
City:	Sonora, Cal.
Value:	$ _____

The soda works was eventually purchased by Michael Terzich also of Sonora.

MILLVILLE GLASS WORKS (Luther Mills')
Location: San Francisco
Face: **MILLVILLE GLASS WORKS**
              L. M. & Co.

Reverse: Blank
Bottom: Iron Pontil Mark
Rarity: Very Rare
Date: 1852 – 1853
Proprietor: Luther Mills
Address: 57 Front Street
City: San Francisco, Ca.
Value: $ _____

Luther Mill's & Co. were established in San Francisco in 1852.

In 1853 the company became known as Luther Mills' & James Vantine dealers & importers of wine & liquors.

Their partnership lasted until 1858. Mills' continued the business and Vantine became partner with Levi Markley in the produce business.

Because of ill health Mill's sold out in 1869 moving to Santa Clara County purchasing the Aperient Springs, changing the name to Mill's Seltzer Springs.

MILL'S (Luther Mills')

Location:	Santa Clara
Face:	MILLS'
	SELTZER
	SPRINGS
Reverse:	Blank
Top:	Applied Double Collar
Bottom:	Blank
Rarity:	Extremely Rare
Date:	1874 - 1885
Proprietor:	Luther Mills
Address:	Santa Clara County
City:	Santa Clara, Ca.
	Formerly the Aperient Springs
Value:	$ _____

MILL'S (Luther Mills')
Location: Santa Clara
Face: **MILLS'**
SELTZER
SPRINGS
Reverse: Blank
Bottom: **M**
Rarity: Scarce
Date: 1874 - 1885
Proprietor: Luther Mills
Address: Santa Clara County
City: Santa Clara, Ca.
Formerly the Aperient Springs
Value: $ _____

Luther Mills purchased the Congress Springs Hotel in 1869 operating it for five years. He then purchased the Aperient Springs in Santa Clara.

He developed the springs changing the name to Mill's Pacific Seltzer Springs, also known as Mills' Seltzer Springs.

He later sold to John Ryland who changed the name to Azule Seltzer Springs.

MISENHEIMER & HALL

Location:	San Jose Area
Face:	**MISENHEIMER & HALL**
	ALMA SODA
Reverse:	Blank
Base:	**PACIFIC GLASS WORKS**
Rarity:	Extremely Rare
Date:	1862-1865
Proprietor:	Misenheimer & Hall
Address:	
City:	Alma Santa Clara County
Value:	$_____

Alma, California is under the Lexington Reservoir in Santa Clara County near San Jose.

This is one of the rarest Western Soda bottles.

MOISE & Co.

Location:	San Francisco
Face:	C. MOISE & Co. SAN FRANCISCO
Reverse:	GENUINE PACIFIC GINGER BEER
Bottom:	Blank
Rarity:	Extremely Rare
Date:	Late 1870's
Proprietor:	C. Moise
Address:	?
City:	San Francisco, Ca.
Value:	$ _____
	Eric McGuire collection

MONIER & Co.

Location:	San Francisco
Face:	J. MONIER & CO.
	CL FR NA
Reverse:	J. MONIER & CO.
	CL FR N
Bottom:	Blank
Rarity:	Rare
Date:	1856 – 1858
Proprietor:	Jerome Monier
Address:	160½ Commercial Street
City:	San Francisco, Ca.
Value:	$ _____

Monier & Co. where also hair dressers at the same location, 160½ Commercial Street in 1856-1857 and moving to 185 Clay Street 1857-1858

MOONEY

Location:	Visalia
Face:	**M. MOONEY**
	VISALIA
Reverse:	Blank
Bottom:	Blank
Rarity:	Rare
Date:	1872 – 1881
Proprietor:	Michael Mooney
Address:	Corner Main & Garden Street
City:	Visalia, Ca.
Value:	$ _____

Michael Mooney operated a brewery in Visalia In 1869 – 1881 corner of Main & Garden Street. Michael died in 1881 and his brother Hugh Continued the business.

M. R. SACRAMENTO

Location:	Sacramento
Face:	M. R. SACRAMENTO
Reverse:	UNION GLASS WORKS PHILADA.
Bottom:	Iron Pontil Mark
Rarity:	Rare
Date:	1851 – 1863
Proprietor:	Martin Rancich
Address:	1851 Grocery Clerk 135 J Street
	1852-1853 Liquor Merchant
	1854-1856 Soda Manufactory
	1856-1860 Fifth near J Street
	1861-1863 19 5th Street
City:	Sacramento, Ca.
Value:	$ _____

MARTIN RANCICH

Location:	Sacramento
Face:	M. R. SACRAMENTO
Reverse:	UNION GLASS WORKS PHILADA
Bottom:	Iron Pontil Mark
Rarity:	Rare
Date:	1851 - 1863
Proprietor:	Martin Rancich
Address:	1851 Grocery Clerk 135 J Street 1852-1853 Liquor Merchant 1854-1856 Soda Manufactory 1856-1860 Fifth near J Street 1861-1863 19 5th Street
City:	Sacramento, Ca.
Value:	$ _____

M. R. & D.
GAETANO DELUCHI

Location:	Sacramento
Face:	M.R.& D.
Reverse:	UNION GLASS WORKS PHILADA
Bottom:	Blank
Rarity:	Extremely Rare
Date:	1863 – 1864
Proprietor:	Gaetano Deluchi & Martin Rancich
Address:	
City:	Sacramento, Ca.
Value:	$ _____

Gaetano Deluchi worked for Martin Rancich in the early 1850's becoming a partner in 1863. They were together until 1864.

Martin Rancich became the proprietor of the Central Restaurant in Sacramento on K Street in 1871.

Gaetano Deluchi became a commission merchant in Sacramento.

MINERAL WATER
Face: **MINERAL**
            WATER
Unnamed favorite bottle of mine
John C. Burton Collection

MT. TAMALPAIS

Location:	San Rafael
Face:	**MT. TAMALPAIS**
	NATURAL
	MINERAL
	WATER CO.
	SAN RAFAEL, CAL.
Reverse:	**A MILD MINERAL WATER**
	TAMALPAIS SODA
	FREE FROM
	ALL DELETERIOUS INGREDIENTS
	TRADE MARK
Bottom:	Blank
Rarity:	Rare
Date:	1906 plus
Proprietor:	Borello Brothers
Address:	
City:	San Rafael, Ca.
Value:	$ _____
	John C. Burton Collection

NAPA SODA W & W S. F.
Location: San Francisco
Face: **NAPA**
SODA
W & W S.F.

Reverse: **NATURAL**
MINERAL WATER
Bottom: Blank
Rare: Extremely rare
Date: 1863
Proprietor: Whitney & Wood
Address:
City: San Francisco, Ca.
Value: $ _____

October 17, 1863
Decision in regard to the **Napa Soda Springs**.
Our readers are aware that the Springs, and the grounds surrounding and adjacent, were claimed by Amos Buckman, who has been litigating for possession of the property for several years past, through the Courts in this State.

Several decisions having been made against Buckman, and in favor of Whitney & Wood. Recently Buckman has set up a pre-emption claim, and the right of ownership to the Government land has lately been decided by the Register and Receiver United States for the San Francisco Land District.

The following in relation to the matter is from the San Francisco Bulletin: The pre-emption claim of Amos Buckman to the **Napa Soda Springs** has been rejected by the U. S. Register and Receiver for this district. They decide, from the testimony, that Buckman never was a settler in good faith, so as to secure the benefits of the preemption law, but was a mere claimant of the land for speculative purposes. Rejecting this claim, they find that the title to the land passed from the United States by virtue of a School-land warrant location made by one **Whitney,** who subsequently conveyed his interest to J. Henry Wood and Charles H. Parker of this city.

NAPA SODA - P & W S. F.

Location: San Francisco
Face: NAPA
             SODA
            P & W S.F.

Reverse: NATURAL
            MINERAL WATER
Bottom: Blank
Rarity: No whole specimens known
Date: 1861-1862
Proprietor: Charles H. Parker & J. Henry Wood
Address:
City: San Francisco, Ca.
Value: $ _____

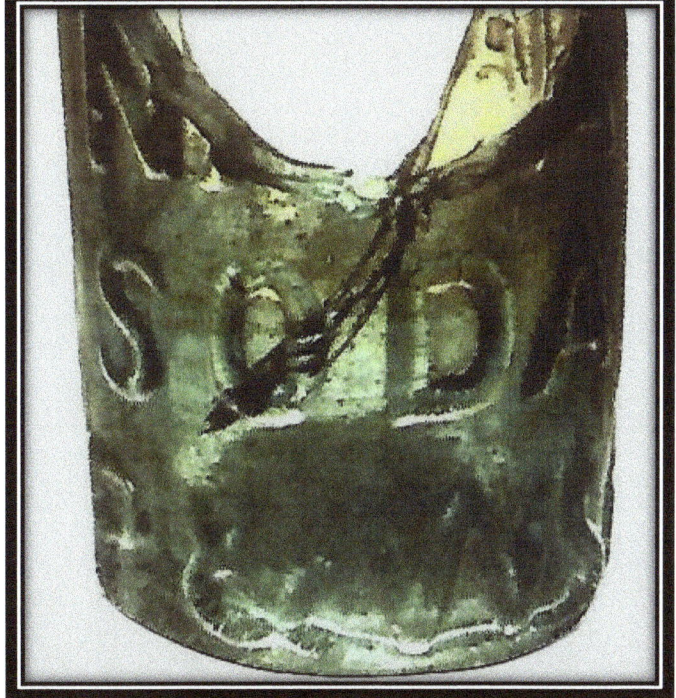

NAPA SODA - WOOD'S

Location:	San Francisco
Face:	NAPA
	SODA
Reverse:	NATURAL
	MINERAL WATER
Bottom:	Blank
Rarity:	Scarce
	Rare in Amber
Date:	1861 - 1873
Proprietor:	(Wood's)
Address:	111 Post Street
	124 Sutter Street
City:	San Francisco, Ca.
Value:	$ _____
	John C. Burton Collection

NAPA WOOD'S STAR SODA

Location:	San Francisco
Face:	**NAPA**
	(Star)
	WOOD'S
	(Star)
	SODA
Bottom:	Blank
Rarity	Very Rare
Date:	1870 - 1872
Proprietor:	Thomas W. Fenn
Address:	111 Post Street
City:	San Francisco, Ca.
Value:	$ _____

1870 – Napa Soda Company
    Office 111 Post Street
    Thomas W. Fenn Agent
    Natural Soda Water

1871 – Napa Soda Company
    Office 124 Sutter Street
    Thomas W. Fenn Agent

1872 – Napa Soda
    Fenn & Burdell Agents
    124 Sutter Street

Front: WOOD'S / NAPA / SODA
Re: NATURAL / MINERAL WATER

Round, Smooth Base
Applied Top
Aqua, $275.00 - 2009
Teal Blue, $500.00 - 2021
Green, Cobalt
Rare
Circa: 1868-1873
Locale: San Francisco
Note: A couple of these were dug in the Benicia Arsenal in 1976, and they have also been dug in Grass Valley.

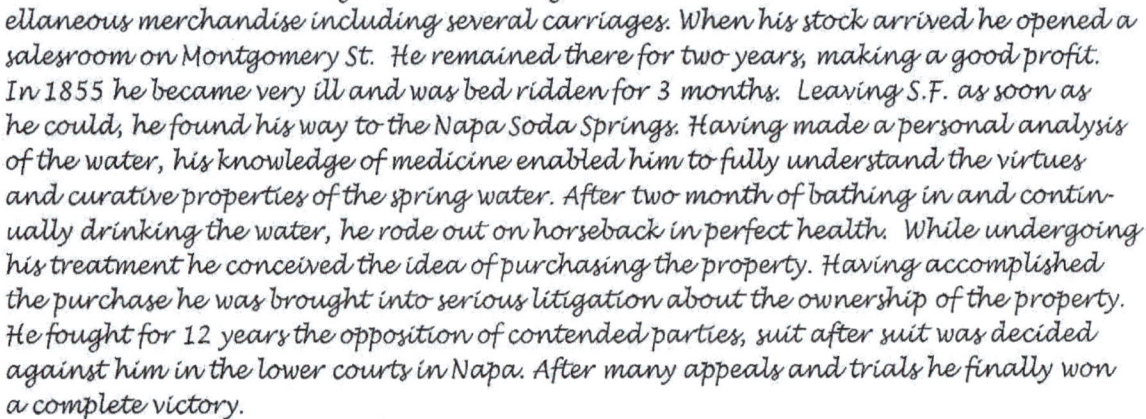

HISTORY: J. Henry Wood was born in New York state in 1818. He was a partner a retail dry goods firm. With his health failing he decided to retire from active business affairs. He concluded he would try the health giving climate of California and left New York in 1853. He brought with him large number is miscellaneous merchandise including several carriages. When his stock arrived he opened a salesroom on Montgomery St. He remained there for two years, making a good profit. In 1855 he became very ill and was bed ridden for 3 months. Leaving S.F. as soon as he could, he found his way to the Napa Soda Springs. Having made a personal analysis of the water, his knowledge of medicine enabled him to fully understand the virtues and curative properties of the spring water. After two month of bathing in and continually drinking the water, he rode out on horseback in perfect health. While undergoing his treatment he conceived the idea of purchasing the property. Having accomplished the purchase he was brought into serious litigation about the ownership of the property. He fought for 12 years the opposition of contended parties, suit after suit was decided against him in the lower courts in Napa. After many appeals and trials he finally won a complete victory.

The property was worth a large amount and in the year 1861, the receiver, who was court appointed, paid Dr. Wood a profit of $12,000.00. The annual income of the springs would increase when, in 1862 Dr. Wood decided to bottle and sell the water for public use. He made many improvements to the springs and surrounding land. He planted a vineyard in 1862, he made the first Hock Wine on the Pacific Coast. He retired from business life in 1872. Dr. Wood trade marked his bottle in 1871, see drawing.. The Napa Soda Springs ad is circa 1870's.

1868-1869 Wood, J. Henry, Proprietor Napa Soda Springs, Office #1 Masonic Temple
1870-1873 Napa Wood Company, depot 122 Berry, Office 418 Montgomery

NAPA SODA - THOMAS A. WHITE

Location:	San Francisco
Face:	NAPA SODA
Reverse:	NATURAL MINERAL WATER T. A. W.
Rarity:	Rare
Date:	1861 – 1862
Proprietor:	Thomas A. White
Address:	512 Washington Street 613 Sansome Street
City:	San Francisco, Ca.
Value:	$ _____

1861 was the first year that Napa Soda Springs was mentioned in a newspaper ad.
Thomas also mentioned he was an agent for Napa Mineral Water in 1862.

NAPA SODA – THOMAS A. WHITE

Location:	San Francisco
Face:	NAPA
	SODA
Reverse:	NATURAL
	MINERAL
	T A W. G. T.
Bottom:	Blank
Rarity:	Rare
Date:	1870 - 1872
Proprietor:	Thomas W. Fenn
Address:	111 Post Street
City:	San Francisco, Ca.
Value:	$ _____
	John C. Burton Collection

NAPA SODA - HAAS BROS.
Location: Napa

Face: NAPA
              SODA

Reverse: HAAS BROS.
              NATURAL
              MINERAL WATER

Bottom: Blank
Rarity: Scarce in blue
Date: 1873 – 1877
Proprietor: David L. Haas
Address:
City: Napa, Ca.
Value $ _____
              John C. Burton Collection

Haas Bros. bottles were used between 1873-1877 when Col. Jackson purchased Napa Soda Springs bottles from the springs were embossed Jackson's.

There is a listing in 1875-1876 stating that Haas Bros. were agents for Napa Soda Depot in Napa. More than likely they were agents for Napa Soda Water in Napa County prior to M. Silva.

NAPA SODA – HAAS BROS.

Location:	Napa
Face:	**NAPA**
	SODA
Reverse:	**HAAS BROS.**
	NATURAL
	MINERAL WATER
Bottom:	Blank
Rarity:	Rare in Green
Date:	1873 – 1877
Proprietor:	David L. Haas
Address:	
City:	Napa, Ca.
Value	$ _____

John C. Burton Collection

NAPA SODA - PHIL CADUC

Location:	Sacramento
Face:	NAPA
	SODA
	PHIL CADUC
Reverse:	NATURAL
	MINERAL WATER
Bottom:	Blank
Rarity:	Common in Aqua
	Rare in Colors
Date:	1873 - 1874
Proprietor:	Phil Caduc
Address:	41 – 43 Third
	Between J & K Streets
	1874-1879
	Agent for Philadelphia Brewery, Napa, and Pacific Congress Water,
	1879-1881
	Napa Soda, ale & Porter, and dealer In coal. 1009-1015 Third Street.
City:	Sacramento, Ca.
Value:	$ _____
	John C. Burton Collection

Phil Caduc was an agent for Napa Soda Water in the Sacramento areas early as 1861. His first bottles were probably marked only NAPA SODA on the face.

When Col. Jackson purchased Nopa Soda Springs Caduc was probably forced to a new bottle design With his name on the bottle.

In 1881 Louis Leloy became the Napa Soda Water agent in Sacramento.

Rick Siri Collection

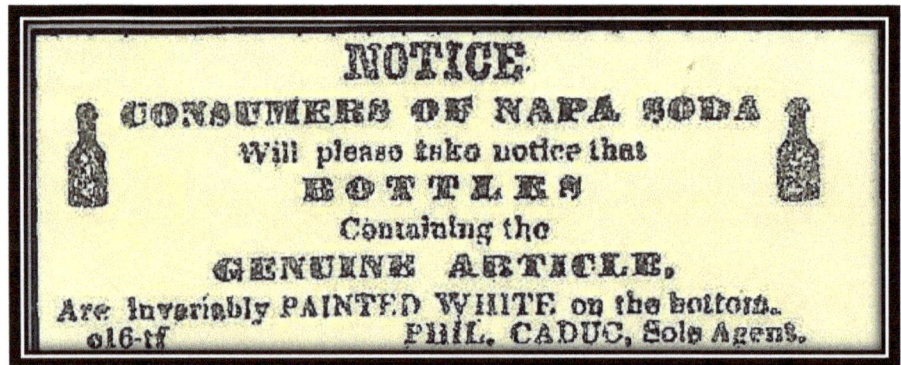

NAPA SODA - LOUIS LELOY

Location:	Sacramento
Face:	**NAPA**
	SODA
	LOUIS LELOY
Reverse:	**NATURAL**
	MINERAL WATER
Bottom:	Blank
Rarity:	Scarce
Date:	1880 - 1884
Proprietor:	Louis Leloy
Address:	22 J Street
	Hair Dresser, Liquor & Cigars
	1881 Agent for Napa Soda Water
City:	Sacramento, Ca.
Value:	$ _____
	John C. Burton Collection

NAPA SODA – B. F. CONNOLLY

Location:	Petaluma, Sonoma County
Face:	**NAPA**
	SODA
	B. F. CONNOLLY
Reverse:	**NATURAL**
	MINERAL WATER
Bottom:	Blank
Rarity:	Rare
Date:	1872 - 1873
Proprietor:	Bernard F. Connolly
Address:	
City:	Petaluma, Cal.
Value:	$ _____
	John C. Burton Collection

Connolly was an agent for Napa Soda in Sonoma County in the early 1870's and previously was known as Connolly & Bro. in San Francisco and the North Bay area.

NEVADA CITY

Location:	Nevada City (Grass Valley Area)
Face:	**NEVADA CITY**
	SODA WORKS
	L. SIEBERT
Reverse:	Blank
Bottom:	Blank
Rarity:	Semi Rare
Date:	1870's – 1880's
Proprietor:	Louis Siebert
Address:	
City:	San Francisco, Ca.
Value:	$ _____

LOUIS SEIBERT'S VINEYARD & SODA WORKS
1880 Thompson & West atlas of Nevada County

NEW ALMADEN

Location:	San Jose
Face:	**NEW ALMADEN**
	MINERAL WATER
	Vertical
Reverse:	**W & W**
Bottom:	Blank
Variant:	1870 on face of bottle
Rarity:	Aqua & Green Extremely Rare
Date:	1854-1861
	Thomas & David Williams
	1862-1872 Winslow & Williams
Proprietor:	Thomas & David Williams
Address:	St. John between First & Market
City:	San Jose, Ca.
Value:	$ _____

THOMAS & David Williams bottled water from springs located at the New Almaden Mines in 1854.

They had purchased the bottling apparatus from Gerriche & Leach.

Registered Trade Mark

NEW ALMADEN

Location:	San Jose
Face:	NEW ALMADEN
	MINL WATER
Reverse:	W & W
Bottom:	Blank
Rarity:	Common in aqua
	Extremely Rare in Blue
Date:	1860 – 1872
Variant:	1870 on face of bottle
Proprietor:	Thomas & David Williams & Winslow
Address:	St. John between First & Market
City:	San Jose, Ca.
Value:	$ _____
	John C. Burton Collection

NEW ALMADEN

Location:	San Francisco
Face:	TRADE (Shield) MARK
	A & P
	NEW ALMADEN
	VICHY WATER
	CALIFORNIA
Reverse:	Blank
Bottom:	Blank
Colors:	Green, Yellowish Green, Teal Green, Amber & Deep Amber

Pint Size Colors: Green & Olive Amber

Rarity:	Extremely Rare
Date:	1869 – 1874
Proprietor:	Walter O. Chauvin agent
Address:	506 Jackson Street
City:	San Francisco, Ca.
Value:	$ 2,800 Green
	$ 3,200 Yellow

Found in both quart & pint sizes with colors being in Amber & Deep Aqua, Teal Green & Yellowish Green.

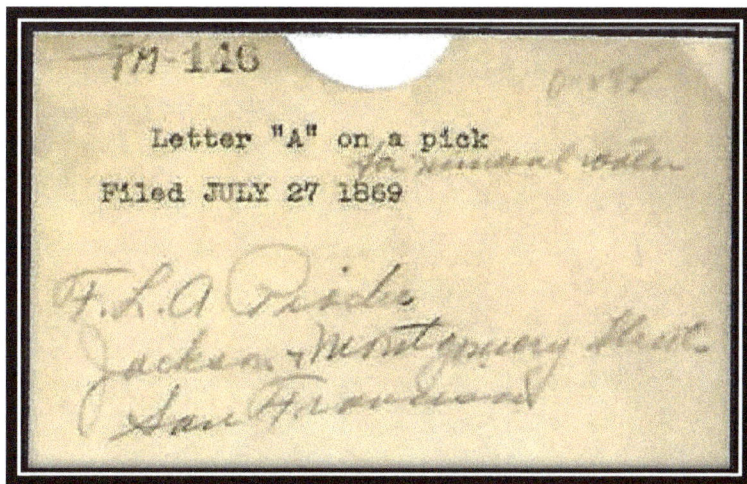

July 1869 Trade Marked by L. A. Pioche

ADDITIONAL NEW ALMADEN VICHY COLORED BOTTLES

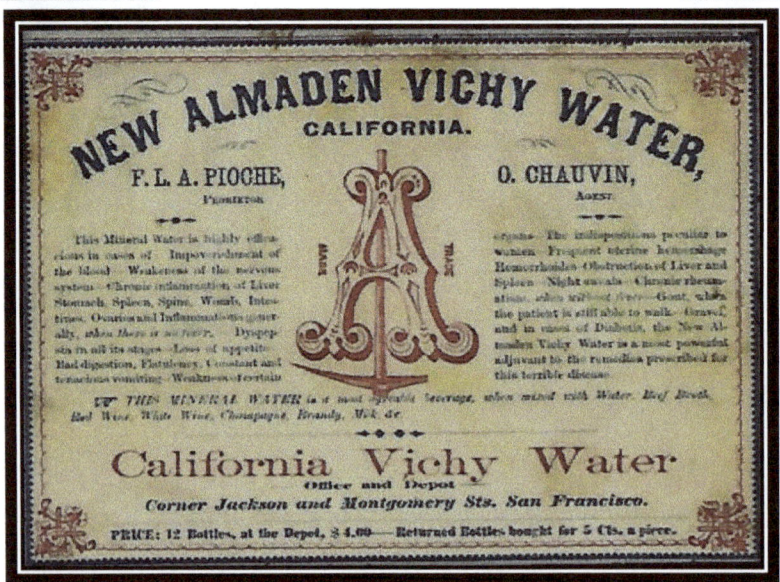

NEW ALMADEN

Location:	Santa Clara County
Face:	NEW ALMADEN
	VICHY WATER
	CALIFORNIA
Reverse:	TRADE (Crest) MARK
	A. P.
Bottom:	Blank
Rarity:	Extremely Rare
A. P. initials:	F. L. A. Pioche
Date:	1870 - 1872
Agent:	Walter O. Chauvin agent
Address:	506 Jackson Street
	1872-1874
Agents:	Chauvin & Onesime
	Office 607 Washington Street
City:	San Francisco, Ca.
Value:	$ 3,600
	Eric McGuire collection

NEW CENTURY

Location:	San Francisco
Face:	**NEW CENTURY MINERAL WATER**
Reverse:	Blank
Bottom:	**P.C.G.W.**
Rarity:	Rare
Date:	1904 – 1910
Proprietor:	Puccinelli & Belli
Address:	713 Laguna Street
City:	San Francisco, Ca.
Value:	$ _____

1904 - Puccinelli & Belli proprietors 713 Laguna Street

1905 - Puccinelli & Belli proprietors 713 Union Street

1906 – New Century Soda Works Co. 3125 Laguna Street

1908 – New Century Soda Works Co. 3209 Laguna Street

1909 – New Century Soda Works Co. 439 Green Street

1910 – San Francisco & New Century Seltzer Co.

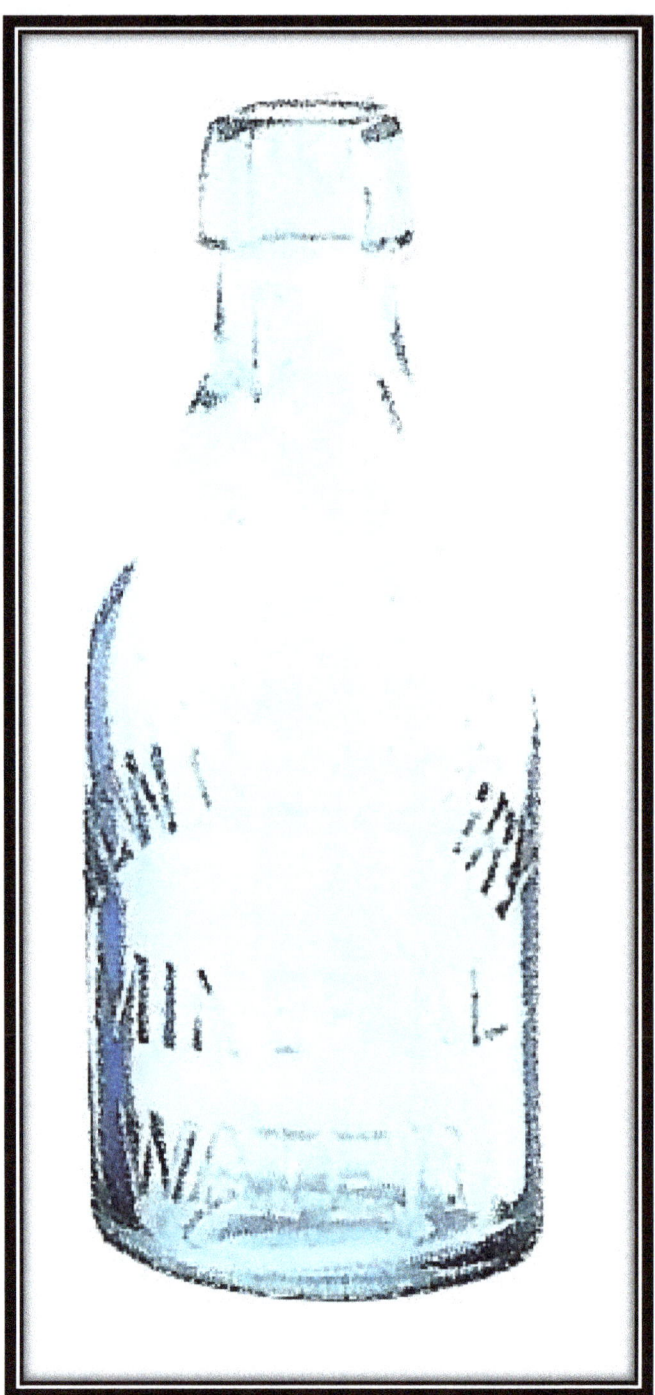

NEW LIBERTY

Location:	San Francisco
Face:	NEW LIBERTY S. W. Co.
	TRADE
	(Head)
	MARK
	S. F.
Reverse:	Blank
Bottom:	Blank
Rarity:	Rare
Date:	1899 – 1902
Proprietor:	Herman Schmidt
Address:	3272 24th Street
City:	San Francisco, Ca.
Value:	$ _____

1899-1900 - New Liberty Soda Water Co.
   Herman Schmidt & Co.
   3272 24th Street
1900-1902 – New Liberty Soda Works
   Herman Schmidt proprietor
   3272 24th Street

NEYMAN & DRAKE

Location:	Mokelumne Hill
Face:	NEYMAN & DRAKE
	MOK HILL
	SODA WORKS
Reverse:	UNION GLASS WORKS
	PHILADA
Bottom:	Blank
Rarity:	Extremely Rare
Date:	1858-1874
Proprietor:	Neyman & Drake
Address:	
City:	Mokelumne Hill
Value	$ _____

Neyman & Drake operated Mok Hill Soda Works until 1874 selling the business to Werle & Albright who changed the name to Pioneer Soda Factory.

NONPAREIL

Location:	San Francisco
Face:	NONPAREIL
	SODA WATER CO.
	S. F.
Reverse:	Blank
Bottom:	B B B
Rarity:	Tooled Top Scarce
	Applied Top Rare
Date:	1881 – 1887
Proprietor:	Samuel Benjamin
Address:	719 – 721 Bryant Street
City:	San Francisco, Ca.
Value:	$ _____

Prior to 1881 Eastern Soda Works was located at 719 – 721 Bryant Street.

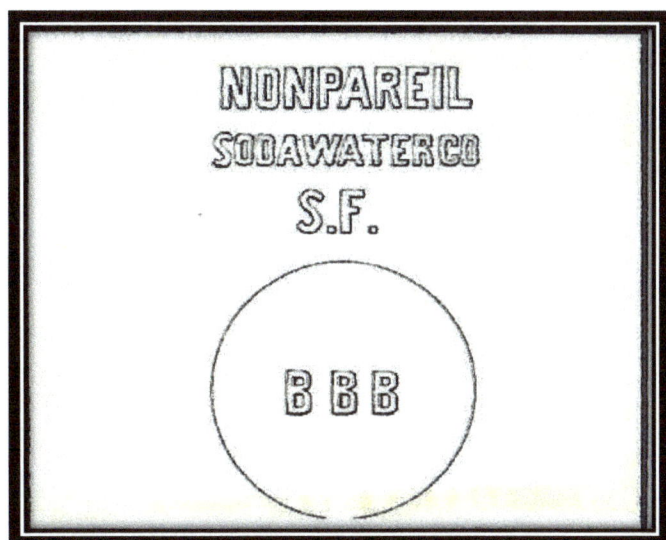

Nonpareil Trade Mark

PACIFIC CONGRESS WATER (Luther Mills – See Pages 149-151)

Location:	Saratoga, Santa Clara County
Face:	PACIFIC
	CONGRESS
	WATER
Reverse:	RUNNING DEER
Bottom:	Blank
Rarity:	Rare
Date:	1869-1871
	Luther Mills Agent
	126 Kearney Street
	1872-1874
	Henry Klein Agent
	126 Kearney Street
	1874-1875 Louis Sage
	1875-1880
	Henry Benjamin & Co. Proprietor
	Natural Mineral Springs Water
	Depot 29 New Montgomery Street
	1881
	James Bliven & D. C. Mitchell
	Proprietors at 29 New Montgomery
City:	San Francisco
Value:	$ _____

188

PACIFIC CONGRESS WATER

Location:	San Francisco
Face:	**PACIFIC CONGRESS WATER**
Reverse:	No deer
Bottom:	Blank
Date:	1869 – 1876
Rarity:	Rare
Proprietor:	Luther R. Mills
Address:	
City:	San Francisco, Ca.
Value:	$ _____

No running deer on back.

PACIFIC CONGRESS WATER

Location:	Sacramento
Face:	PACIFIC CONGRESS WATER
Reverse:	PHIL CADUC
Bottom:	Blank
Rarity:	Scarce
Date:	1868 – 1881
Agent:	Phil Caduc
Address:	
City:	Sacramento, Cal.
Value:	$ _____

Vertical Print

PACIFIC CONGRESS WATER – SAGE'S

Location:	San Francisco
Face:	**SAGE'S**
	PACIFIC CONGRESS
	WATER
Reverse:	Blank
Bottom:	Blank
Rarity:	Rare
Date:	1874 - 1875
Agent:	Louis A. Sage & Henry W. Klein
Address:	162 Montgomery Street
City:	San Francisco, Ca.
Value:	$ _____

PACIFIC CONGRESS WATER SPRINGS SARATOGA

Location:	Southwest of San Jose, Santa Clara County
Face:	PACIFIC CONGRESS WATER SPRINGS SARATOGA
	(Deer)
	CALIFORNIA
Reverse:	PACIFIC CONGRESS
	SPRINGS
Year:	Circa 1870's
Rarity:	Extremely Rare

Double Collar

PACIFIC CONGRESS SPRING SARATOGA

PACIFIC CONGRESS SPRINGS

Notice the difference in tops

PACIFIC GLASS WORKS

Location:	San Francisco
Face:	Blank
Reverse:	Blank
Bottom:	**PACIFIC GLASS WORKS**
Colors:	Light Blue & Dark Green
Rarity:	Rare
Date:	1863 – 1864
	Pacific Glass Works
	Corner Iowa & Mariposa
	Office 621 Clay Street
	1865-1866
	Corner Mariposa Near Mississippi
	1867-1874
	Bennett & Co. Proprietors
	Corner Mariposa & Iowa
	Office 514 Washington Street
	1875-1876
	John Taylor & R. K. Pattridge
	John Taylor & Co. Agents
	Office 514 Washington Street
	1876
	Pacific Glass Works merged with
	San Francisco Glass Works becoming
	San Francisco & Pacific Glass Works
	Proprietor:
City:	San Francisco, Ca.
Value:	$ _____

JOHN TAYLOR & CO.
512 AND 514 WASHINGTON STREET,
IMPORTERS OF AND DEALERS IN
DRUGGISTS' GLASSWARE
AND SUNDRIES,

The latest styles of Glassware and Fixtures for first-class Drug Stores, with Glass Labels, Counter and Prescription Scales, Druggists' Sundries, Perfumery and Liquor Labels in good variety.

ASSAYERS' MATERIALS AND CHEMICALS.

Bullion and Assay Balances, French and Sand Crucibles,
Humid Assay Apparatus, Dixon's Celebrated Black Lead Crucibles,
Cupelling Furnaces, And everything required in an Assay Office.

PHOTOGRAPHIC GOODS.

We have purchased Mr. Wm. Shew's Entire Stock of Photographic Materials and Chemicals, and have now the most complete and desirable stock of goods in this line in the city, which we are selling at low prices.

Agents of PACIFIC GLASS WORKS

Embossed on bottom

PACIFIC SODA WORKS

Location:	San Francisco
Face:	PACIFIC SODA WORKS
Reverse:	Blank
Bottom:	Blank
Rarity:	Rare
Date:	1853-1868
Address:	Corner Jessie & Jane Streets
Proprietor:	D. A. Mowry
Date:	1868 – 1869
Proprietor:	John F. Rohe
Address:	115 Jesse Street
	1869-1870
	1112 Market Street
City:	San Francisco, Ca.
Value:	$ _____
	John C. Burton Collection

F. PAILLET

Location:	San Francisco
Face:	F. PAILLET NATURAL MINERAL WATER S. F.
Reverse:	NATURAL MINERAL WATER FROM THE GOLDEN WEST SPRINGS NAPA COUNTY, CAL.
Bottom:	Blank
Rarity:	Rare
Date:	1901 – 1906
Proprietor:	Frank Paillet
Address:	820 Buchanan 1609 O'Farrell
City:	San Francisco, Ca.
Value:	$ _____
	John C. Burton Collection

Until 1901 Peter Somps & Frank Paillet had been partners at Golden West Soda Works located at 624 Laguna Street. Paillet moved to Buchanan.

198

PEARSONS SODA WORKS

Location:	Placerville
Face:	**PEARSON'S SODA WORKS**
Reverse:	Blank
Bottom:	Blank
Rarity:	Scarce
Date:	1870's
Proprietor:	John McFarland Pearson
Address:	Ice House
City:	Placerville, Ca.
Value:	$ _____

John C. Burton Collection

1852 John Pearson Soda Works Placerville
1890 John Pearson Jr. Soda Works Placerville
1917 Mrs. John Pearson Jr. Soda Works Placerville
1920 Sold to Scheerer Bros. Placerville
1936 Sold to R. A. Hook Placerville Coca Cola Agent

1876 Pearson Bros. started Soda Works in Carson City
Located on South Carson & Fifth Streets
1881 Soda Works in Carson City closed because of law suits

1880 Opened Soda Works in Bodie, California
1883 Sold Bodie Soda Works and returned to Placerville

PHILLIP'S

Location:	San Francisco
Face:	**PHILLIPS**
	NAPA
	CO.
	SODA
Reverse:	**PHILLIP'S**
	SODA SPRINGS
	NATURAL
	MINERAL WATER
Bottom:	Blank
Rarity:	Common
Date:	1899 – 1900
	Formerly Walter's Napa Soda
Proprietor:	Samuel A. Phillips
Address:	717 McAllister Street
	1900-1901
	2037 15th Street
1901	Phillips & I. H. Spiro Co.
City:	San Francisco, Ca.
Value:	$ _____

PHILLIP'S

Location:	San Francisco
Face:	PHILLIP'S
	NAPA
	CO.
	SODA
Reverse:	PHILLIP'S
	SODA SPRINGS
	NATURAL
	MINERAL WATER
Bottom:	Blank
Rarity:	Scarce
Date:	1899 – 1901
Proprietor:	Samuel A. Phillips
Address:	717 McAllister Street
City:	San Francisco, Ca
Value:	$ _____

John C. Burton Collection

PIONEER SODA WORKS

Location:	San Francisco
Face:	**PIONEER**
	(Bear)
	SODA WATER CO.
	S. F.
Reverse:	Blank
Bottom:	Blank
Rarity:	Rare
Date:	1896-1897
	William Welch & George Collins
	1897 – 1902
Proprietor:	Martin & Charles Welch
	1902-1906
	Louis Thierback
Address:	1555 Mission Street
City:	San Francisco, Ca.
Value:	$ _____

1896-1897 William Welch & George Collins were owners of Pioneer Soda Water Works. They sold to Martin & Charles Welch in 1897 who changed the name to Pioneer Soda Water Co.

The Welch brothers sold to Louis Thierback in 1902 who operated it until 1906. Earthquake?

There was also a Pioneer Soda Works at 21 & 22 Hinckley Street from 1878 to 1882 owned by Henry Wiggett & Charles Lupton. Listed as manufacturers of Ginger Beer & Soda Water.

PIONEER SODA WORKS

Location:	San Francisco
Face:	PIONEER SODA WATER SAN FRANCISCO
Reverse:	Blank
Bottom:	T
Rarity:	Common
Date:	1854-1858
Proprietor:	Cephas Turner
Address:	Rear of 280 Dupont Street (Now Grant Avenue) 1858-1863 Peter Brader & John Rohe 1863- 1865 James Bliven & Fitzpatrick 529 Jackson Street 1866-1872 Turner & Fitzpatrick 1873 Turner & Fitzpatrick worked for Bay City Soda Works
City:	San Francisco, Ca.
Value:	$ _____

PIONEER SODA WORKS

Location:	San Francisco
Face:	**PIONEER**
	SODA WORKS
	PSW in shield
Reverse:	Blank
Bottom:	Blank
Rarity:	Rare in Colors
Date:	1877 - 1896
Proprietor:	Martin Walch & Charles Welch
	And Raymo Angelo
Address:	1719½ Market Street
City:	San Francisco, Ca.
Value:	$ _____

PIONEER SODA WORKS

Location:	San Francisco
Face:	PIONEER
	SODA WORKS
	TRADE (Shield) MARK
Reverse:	Blank
Bottom:	Blank
Rarity:	Common in Aqua
	Scarce in Colors
Date:	1877 - 1896
Proprietor:	Martin & Charles Welch
Address:	1719½ Market Street
City:	San Francisco, Ca.
Value:	$ _____

Some have "W" in shield

PRIEST'S NAPA

Location:	St. Helena
Face:	PRIEST
	NAPA
Reverse:	NATURAL
	BOTTLED
	AT THE
	SPRINGS
	MINERAL WATER
Bottom:	Blank
Rarity:	Common in Aqua
Date:	1883-1897
Proprietor:	Joshua J. Priest
	1883-1906
	D. C. Priest
City:	Napa, Ca.
Value:	$ _____
	John C. Burton Collection

Priest Soda Springs are located in Priest Canyon, Napa County near St. Helena.

PRIEST NAPA

Location:	St. Helena
Face:	**PRIEST**
	NAPA
Reverse:	**NATURAL**
	MINERAL WATER
	RECARBONATED
	FROM
	NAPA
	VALLEY CAL.
	THIS BOTTLE NEVER
	SOLD
Bottom:	**366 H**
Rarity:	Scarce
Date:	1883-1897
Proprietor:	Joshua J. Priest
	1897-1906
	D. C. Priest
Value:	$ _____
	John C. Burton Collection

PRIEST'S NATURAL SODA

Location:	St. Helena
Face:	PRIEST'S NATURAL SODA
Reverse:	NATURAL BOTTLED AT THE SPRINGS MINERAL WATER
Bottom:	366 H
Rarity:	Scarce
Date:	1883-1897
Proprietor:	Joshua J. Priest 1897-1906 D. C. Priest
City:	Napa, Ca.
Value:	$ _____

John C. Burton Collection

PRIEST'S NATURAL SODA

Location:	St. Helena
Face:	PRIEST'S NATURAL SODA
Reverse:	NATURAL (Man) MINERAL WATER
Bottom:	Blank
Rarity:	Semi Common
Date:	1883-1897
Proprietor:	Joshua J. Priest
	1897-1906
	D. C. Priest
Value:	$ _____

John C. Burton Collection

PRIEST SODA

Location:	St. Helena
Face:	**PRIEST**
	SODA
Reverse:	**NATURAL**
	(Man)
	MINERAL WATER
Bottom:	Blank
Rarity:	Very Scarce
Date:	1883-1897
Proprietor:	Joshua J. Priest
	1897-1906
	D. C. Priest
Value:	$ _____

PRIEST NAPA VALLEY SODA

Location:	St. Helena
Face:	PRIEST
	NAPA
	VALLEY
	SODA
Reverse:	NATURAL
	MINERAL WATER
	RECARBONATED
	FROM
	NAPA
	VALLEY CAL.
	THIS BOTTLE NEVER
	SOLD
Bottom:	366 H
Rarity:	Semi Scarce
Date:	1883-1897
Proprietor:	Joshua J. Priest
	1897-1906
	D. C. Priest
Value:	$ _____
	John Louder Collection

C. A. REINERS & COMPANY

Location: San Francisco
Face: C. A. REINERS & CO.
SAN
FRANCISCO

Reverse: IMPROVED
TRADE MARK
(Moon & Stars)
MINERAL WATER

Bottom: Blank
No Address
Rarity: Common in Aqua
Rare in Green
Date: 1873 - 1875
Proprietor: C. A. Reiners
723 Turk Street
City: San Francisco, Ca.
Value: $ _____

C. A. Reiners was a partner with H\John Breig at the Eureka Soda Works in 1872.

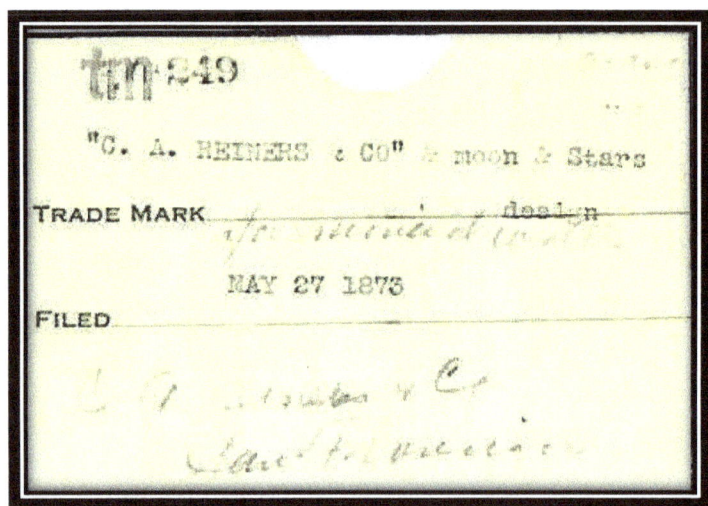

C. A. REINERS & COMPANY

Location:	San Francisco
Face:	C. A. REINERS & CO.
Reverse:	IMPROVED TRADE MARK (Moon & Stars) MINERAL WATER
Bottom:	Blank
Rarity:	Common in Aqua Rare in green
Date:	1875- 1882
Proprietor:	C. A. Reiners 541-543 Bryant Street 1875-1882 723 Turk Street
City:	San Francisco, Ca.
Value:	$

ADDITIONAL REINER'S & CO. COLOR BOTTLES

SAMUEL'S

Location:	Napa
Face:	SAMUEL'S
	NAPA
	SPRING'S
Reverse:	NATURAL
	MINERAL WATER
Bottom:	Blank
Date:	1886 – 1906
Rarity:	Common
Proprietor:	E. C. Samuels
Address:	
City:	Napa, Ca.
Value:	$ _____
	John C. Burton Collection

Near the edge of Lake Berryessa, Napa County.
Comes with the following initials on bottles.

"A" in square
"A" in triangle
"A" is for W. T. Alexander

"A. & B."
"A. & B." is for Alexander & Brown

"M" in triangle with "S. O" on base

"M" in triangle with "E. S." on base
"E.S" for E. S. Samuels

"M" in triangle with "M' on base
"M" is for A. R. J. Morriss

"G" in triangle with "G' on base
"G" is for George H. Gregory
Agent for San Joaquin County

SAMUEL'S

Location:	Napa
Face:	SAMUEL'S
	NAPA
	SPRING'S
Reverse:	NATURAL
	MINERAL WATER
	A & E
Bottom:	G
Rarity:	Semi Rare with "A & E"
Date:	1886 - 1906
Proprietor:	E. C. Samuels
Address:	
City:	Napa, Ca.
Value:	$ _____
	John Louder Collection

216

SAMUEL'S

Location:	Napa

Face:	SAMUEL'S
	  NAPA
	  SODA
	SPRING'S

Reverse:	NATURAL MINERAL WATER A & B
Bottom:	Blank
Rarity:	Scarce with "A & B"
Date:	1886 - 1906
Proprietor:	E. C. Samuels
Address:	
City:	Napa, Ca.
Value:	$ _____

John C. Burton Collection

SAMUEL'S

Location:	Napa
Face:	**SAMUEL'S**
	SODA
	TRADE {A} MARK
	SPRING'S
Reverse:	**NATURAL**
	MINERAL WATER
Bottom:	Blank
Rarity:	Semi Rare with "A"
Date:	1886 - 1906
Proprietor:	E. C. Samuels
Address:	
City:	Napa, Ca.
Value:	$ _____

218

SAMUEL'S

Location:	Napa
Face:	SAMUEL'S
	SODA
	TRADE (M) MARK
	SPRING'S
Reverse:	NATURAL
	MINERAL WATER
Bottom:	E. S.
Rarity:	Dime a dozen with "M"
Date:	1886 - 1906
Proprietor:	E. C. Samuels
Address:	
City:	Napa, Ca.
Value:	$ _____
	John C. Burton Collection

SAMUEL'S

Location:	Napa
Face:	SAMUEL'S
	SODA
	TRADE (M) MARK
	SPRING'S
Reverse:	NATURAL
	MINERAL WATER
Bottom:	S. O.
Rarity:	Semi Rare with "S. & O."
Date:	1886 - 1906
Proprietor:	E. C. Samuels
Address:	
City:	Napa, Ca.
Value:	$ _____
	John C. Burton Collection

SAN FRANCISCO GLASS WORKS

Location:	San Francisco
Face:	SAN FRANCISCO GLASS WORKS
Reverse:	Blank
Bottom:	Blank
Rarity:	Common in aqua Deep aqua rare Rare in colors
Date:	1870 - 1876
Proprietor:	Newman & Duval
Address:	So. Side King near Fourth Office 313 Montgomery 1875-1876 Office 530 Washington Street 1876
Proprietor:	Carlton Newman Merged with Pacific Glass Works
City:	San Francisco, Ca.
Value:	$ _____

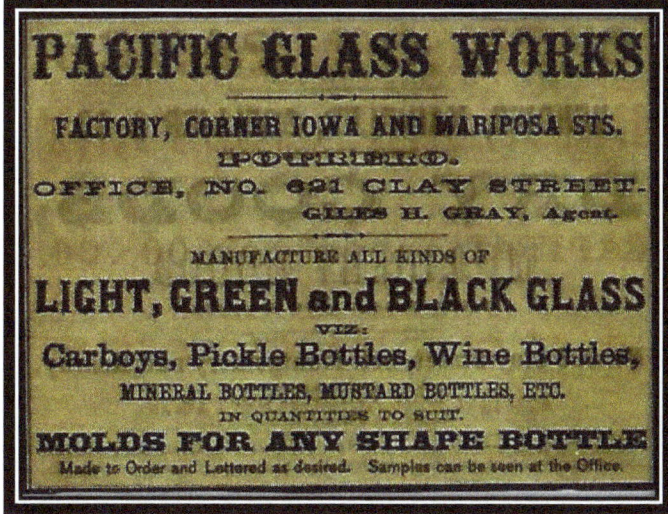

SAN FRANCISCO GLASS WORKS

San Francisco Glass Works
ESTABLISHED 1865.

CARLTON NEWMAN, PROPRIETOR

Office and Works, KING ST., near FOOT OF FOURTH, San Francisco.

Manufacturer of all kinds of GREEN AND BLACK GLASSWARE.
ALL KINDS OF PLAIN AND LETTERED BOTTLES Furnished at short Notice.

SAN JOSE SODA WORS (Works misspelt)

Location:	San Jose
Face:	SAN JOSE
	SODA WORS
	CAL.
Reverse:	Blank
Bottom:	Blank
Rarity:	Scarce
Date:	Late 1870's -1886
Proprietor:	George Stenger
Address:	350 Park Avenue
City:	San Jose, Ca.
Value:	$ _____

SAN LUIS OBISPO

Location:	San Luis Obispo
Face:	SAN LUIS OBISPO
	SODA WATER
	WORKS
	S. CERIBELLI
Reverse:	Blank
Bottom:	Blank
Rarity:	Scarce
Date:	1874 - 1882
Proprietor:	S. Ceribelli
Address:	Monterey Street
	1883
Address:	L. Martin
	Higuera Street
City:	San Luis Obispo, Ca.
Value:	$ _____

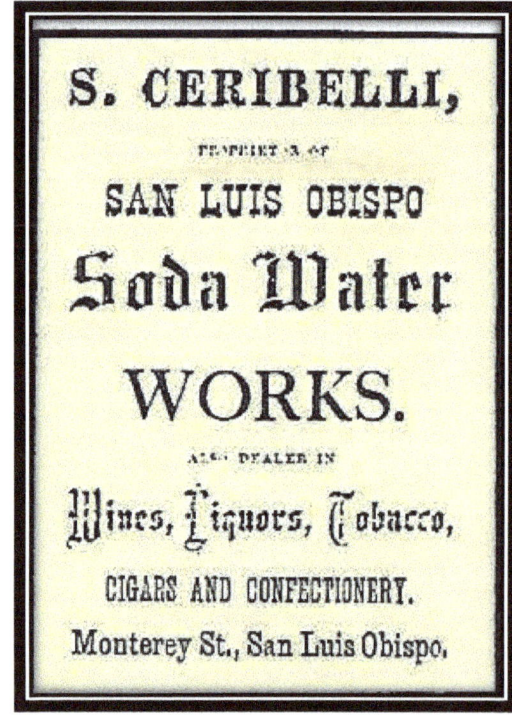

SAN RAFAEL

Location:	San Rafael
Face:	SAN RAFAEL
	SODA WORKS
	L. KAPPERMAN
	PROP'TS
Reverse:	Blank
Bottom:	Blank
Rarity:	Extremely Rare
Date:	1879-1880
Proprietor:	Joseph Kapperman
Address:	Corner 4th & H Streets
City:	San Rafael, Ca.
Value:	$ _____

American Bottle Auctions Image

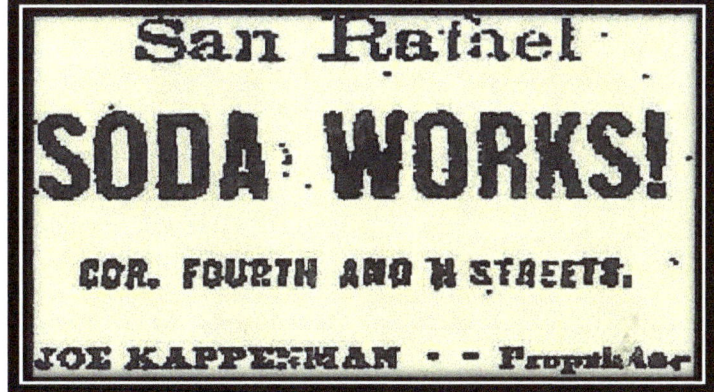

SAN RAFAEL

Location:	San Rafael
Face:	SAN RAFAEL
	SODA WORKS
	P & B
	PROP'TS
Reverse:	Blank
Bottom:	Blank
Rarity:	Extremely Rare
Date:	1880- 1885
Proprietor:	Alphonse Bresson & Sylvan Provencal
Address:	
City:	San Rafael, Ca.
Value:	$ _____

C. SCHNEER – CAPITAL BOTTLING WORKS

Location:	Sacramento
Face:	**NATURAL MINERAL WATER**
	C. SCHNEER & Co.
	SACRAMENTO
	SOLE BOTTLERS
Reverse:	Blank
Bottom:	Blank
Rarity:	Rare
Date:	Prior to 1892
Proprietor:	Constant Schneer & Henry Postel
	1892 - 1906
	Constant, Edward & Antone Schneer
Address:	310 K Street
	1113 Front Street
City:	Sacramento, Ca.
Value:	$ _____

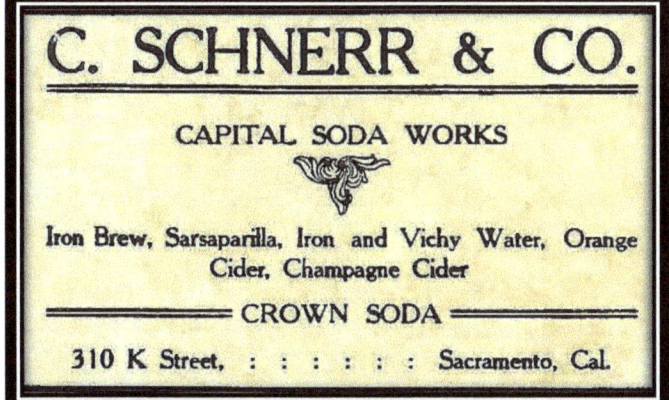

SOMPS & MEILLETTE – EMPIRE SODA WORKS

Location:	Alameda
Face:	J. SOMPS & J. MEILLETTE
	AGENTS
	COR. OAK AND
	BUENA VISTA AVE.
	ALAMEDA
Reverse:	NATURAL
	MINERAL WATER
	FROM THE
	GOLDEN WEST SPRINGS
	NAPA
	COUNTY CAL.
Bottom:	Blank
Rarity:	Extremely Rare
Date:	1892 - 1895
Proprietor:	Jules S. Somps & Jean Meillette
	1895
	Jules & Peter Somps
Address:	2301 Buena Vista corner Oak
City:	Alameda, Ca.
Value:	$ _____

P. SOMPS

Location:	San Francisco
Face:	P. SOMPS
	MINERAL WATER
	NAPA COUNTY
	CAL.
Reverse:	Blank
Bottom:	Blank
Rarity:	Rare
Date:	1901 - 1906
Proprietor:	Peter Somps
Address:	624 Laguna Street
City:	San Francisco, Ca.
Value:	$ _____
	Eric McGuire Collection

Peter Somps purchased the Golden West Soda Works from Pierre Somps & Frank Paillet around 1900.

SUMMIT

Location:	Sacramento
Face:	SUMMIT
	MINERAL WATER
	J. H.
Reverse:	Blank
Bottom:	Blank
Rarity:	Scarce in Aqua
	Rare in Green
Date:	1871 - 1881
Proprietor:	Jacob Hoen
Address:	149 I Street between 5th & 6th
City:	Sacramento, Ca.
Value:	$ _____

Listed as an agent for Summit Ice Company, Pacific Ice Company, Rocky Mountain Coal Company and Summit Mineral Water, Jacob Hoen was a busy man.

1881-1883 he was listed as superintendent not as an agent for Summit.

SUMMIT ICE COMPANY,
JACOB HOEHN, Agent.
Office, 149 I Street, bet. Fifth and Sixth, Sacramento.
ALSO,
Agent for the SUMMIT MINERAL WATER, and ROCKY MOUNTAIN COAL COMPANY.

TAHOE

Location:	Lake Tahoe
Face:	TAHOE
	SODA
	SPRINGS
Reverse:	NATURAL
	MINERAL WATER
Bottom:	Blank
Rarity:	Rare
Date:	1880's
Proprietor:	
Address:	Carnelian Bay North Shore
City:	Lake Tahoe, Placer County
Value:	$ _____

TAYLOR & COMPANY

Location:	San Francisco
Face:	**TAYLOR & Co.**
	SODA WATER
	SAN FRANCISCO
	EUREKA
Reverse:	Blank
Bottom:	Iron Pontil Mark
Rarity:	Very Rare
Date:	1851-1852
Proprietor:	William H. Taylor
	James P. Bradish &
	Charles J. Stokes
Address:	Corner Jessie & Jane
City:	San Francisco, Ca.
Value:	$ _____

The partnership was dissolved April 2, 1852 and continued in business by William H. Taylor.

TAYLOR & COMPANY – VALPARAISO CHILI

Location:	San Francisco
Face:	TAYLOR & Co.
	VALPARAISO
	CHILE
Reverse:	SODA
	WATER
Bottom:	Iron Pontil Mark
Date:	1850's
Rarity:	Scarce in green
	Extremely Rare in Cobalt
Proprietor:	Asher S. Taylor
Address:	Corner Jessie & Jane
City:	San Francisco
Value:	$ _____

Between 1850 and 1852, Asher S. Taylor travelled numerous times by ship to Valparaiso from San Francisco. It is speculated that Asher had bottles blown in the east, had them shipped to Valparaiso, Chili, filled then shipped to San Francisco and/or Sacramento for distribution.

Listed in 1854, Asher Taylor Soda Water Factory on Jesse Street in San Francisco. In 1857, he was employed by Boley Soda Works in Sacramento.

No listing from 1858 to 1860. Is it possible he returned to Valparaiso at this time?

1861-1862 he has returned to Sacramento in the soda business, leaving Sacramento in 1862 moving to San Francisco apparently working for the Connolly Brothers at 222 Front Street.

Being nomadic, he returned to Sacramento from 1863 to 1869. He is listed as a bitters manufacturer in 1870 at O & 11th Streets in Sacramento. He then returned to San Francisco as an agent and manufacturer of Sparkling Medicated Bitters at 1806 Powell Street.

1886 he became a drayman.

The question is, where the bottles shipped to San Francisco by mistake or did he ship and sell them in San Francisco as a marketing venture?

TAYLOR & CO. VALPARAISO, CHILI

TAYLOR & CO. VALPARAISO, CHILI

ASHER S. TAYLOR

This bottle is from Taylor's New York City business from 1847 to 1848. He came around the horn to set up a Western soda business in 1849 and must have brought some of his Eastern bottles and soda water apparatus with him.

Only two are known and both dug up about 2010 in the vicinity of the Monterey Customs House. Taylor went on to begin the Taylor & Co. Valparaiso Chili soda company although nobody is sure if his office was San Francisco or Sacramento. San Francisco seems like the logical choice.

Mike Southworth Collection

TOLENAS SPRINGS

Location:	San Francisco
Face:	TOLENAS
	SODA
	SPRINGS
Reverse:	NATURAL
	MINERAL WATER
Bottom:	Blank
Rarity:	Aqua Common
	Green Rare
Date:	1885-1886
Proprietor:	John C. Remington Agent
Address:	217 Commercial Street
	1887-1900
	Charles Eggars & Sidney S. Gould
	1308 Mission Street
	1900-1906
	Tolenas Mineral Water Co.
	1123 Howard Street
City:	San Francisco, Ca.
Value:	$ _____

In the early 1900's Tolenas Soda Water Co. had an agency in Sacramento at 821 K Street which may account for the "T Bros." on the base.

UNION SODA WORKS

Location:	San Francisco
Face:	UNION SODA WORKS
(Vertical)	"ACID BOTTLE"
	SAN FRANCISCO
Reverse:	THOMPSON'S
	PREMIUM
	MINERAL WATER
Bottom:	Blank
Rarity:	Extremely Rare
Date:	1872 - 1895
Proprietor:	George C. Thompson
Address:	
City:	San Francisco, Ca.
Value:	$ _____

VICHY SPRINGS

Location:	San Francisco
Face:	**VICHY SPRINGS**
	NAPA CO.
	CAL.
Reverse:	**NATURAL**
	MINERAL WATER
Bottom:	S. F.
Rarity:	Common
Date:	1898 - 1906
Proprietor:	Leonce C. Bertin & Constantine Lepori
Address:	520 – 522 Washington St.
City:	San Francisco, Ca.
Value:	$ _____
	John C. Burton Collection

VICHY SPRINGS

Location:	San Francisco
Face:	**VICHY SPRINGS**
	NAPA CO.
	CAL.
Reverse:	**YOUNG'S**
	NATURAL
	MINERAL WATER
Bottom:	S. F.
Rarity:	Common
Date:	1898 - 1906
Proprietor:	Leonce C. Bertin & Constantine Lepori
Address:	520 – 522 Washington St.
City:	San Francisco, Ca.
Value:	$ _____
	John C. Burton Collection

VERNON MINERAL WATER

Face:	**VERNON MINERAL WATER**
Reverse:	Blank
Bottom:	Blank
Rarity:	Unique
Date:	1874-1875
Proprietor:	Joshia Sessions Oakland, Cal.
Agent:	Isacc Kenney 237 Montgomery Street 1875-1878 William H. & Nestel Bovee 238 Washington Street
City:	San Francisco, Ca.
Value:	$ _____

The spring was located in Oakland on the property Of a farmer, Joshia Sessions. He bottled the water And sold it in San Francisco.

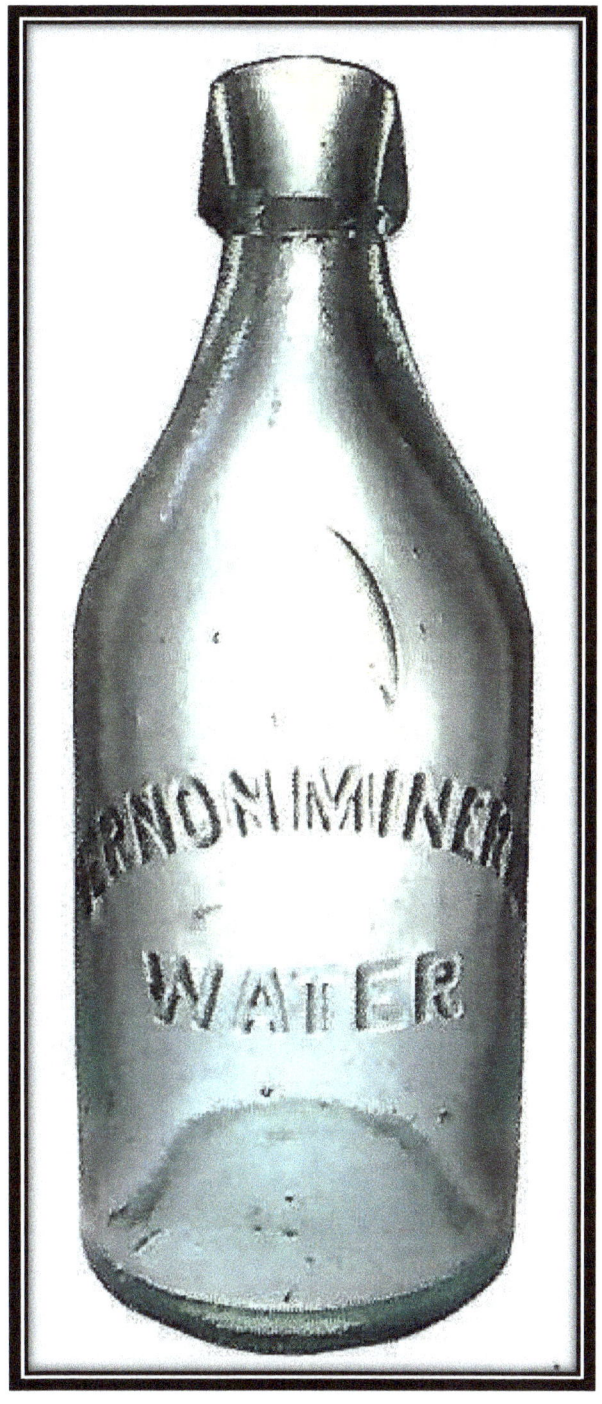

WALTER'S SODA

Location: San Francisco
Face: WALTER'S
                          NAPA
              TRADE (Horseshoe) MARK
                          COUNTY
                          SODA

Reverse: MINERAL WATER
                          FROM
                          WALTER'S
                          SODA
                          SPRINGS

Bottom: HERVE & SOMPS AGTS.
Rarity: Very Common
Date: 1890 - 1891
Proprietor: E. F. Herve & Pierre G. Somps
Address: 114 Stockton Street
City: San Francisco, Ca.
Value: $ _____
              John C. Burton Collection

Golden West Spring's Water came from Walter's Springs.

W. & B. SHASTA

Location:	Shasta
Face:	W & B
	SHASTA
Reverse:	UNION GLASS WORKS PHILAD
	SUPERIOR MINERAL WATER
Bottom:	Iron Pontil Mark
Date:	Early 1850 – 1857
Rarity:	Extremely Rare
Proprietor:	S. B. Westcott & B. L. Bartlett
Address:	Office at 13 Front Street
	Sacramento, Cal.
Value:	$ 14,000

In 1857 Wescott & Bartlett listed the soda works for sale. They were offering 1/3 or 1/2 of the business. Apparently, A. W. Cudworth may have also been a partner as there is reference to Cudworth.

WILLIAMS & SEVERANCE

Location:	San Francisco
Face:	WILLIAMS
	&
	SEVERANCE
Reverse:	Blank
Bottom:	Iron Pontil Mark
Rarity:	Rare with Iron Pontil
	Extremely Rare with Open Pontil
	Extra Rare in Green
Date:	1852 - 1854
Proprietor:	Lewis Williams & Henry Severance
Address:	Vallejo between Stockton & Dupont
City:	San Francisco, Ca.
Value:	$ _____

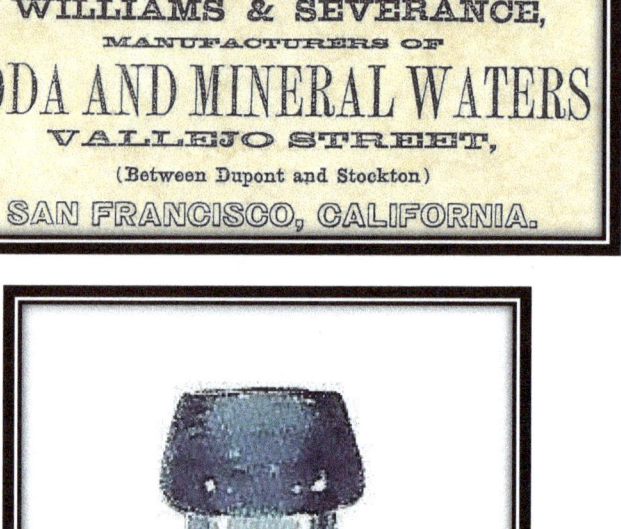

Partnership dissolved October 1853

WILLIAMS & SEVERANCE

Location:	San Francisco
Face:	WILLIAMS
	SEVERANCE
	SAN FRANCISCO
	CAL.
Reverse:	SODA
	MINERAL WATER
Bottom:	Iron Pontil Mark

Rare with Iron Pontil
Extremely Rare with Open Pontil
Extra Rare in Green

Date:	1852 - 1854
Proprietor:	Lewis Williams & Henry Severance
Address:	Vallejo between Stockton & Dupont
City:	San Francisco, Ca.
Value:	$ _____
Variant:	Whiskey Top

WILLIAMS/SEVERANCE/SAN FRANCISCO/CAL.
Rick Siri Collection

HENRY WINKLE

Location:	Sacramento
Face:	**HENRY WINKLE**
	SAC. CITY
Reverse:	X X
Bottom:	Iron Pontil Mark
Date:	1852 – 1854
Rarity:	Scarce with Iron Pontil
	Extremely Rare with open Pontil
Proprietor:	Henry Winkle
Address:	
City:	Sacramento, Ca.
Value:	$ _____

Was Henry Winkle ever in the soda business? See the story on the next page.

HENRY WINKLE

It is speculated that Henry Winkle may not have been in the soda water business but the question is, why so many bottles with his name on them? Winkle was in Sacramento in the early 1850's in the restaurant and bakery business. Apparently, he was also a part-time realtor.

November 2, 1852 Sacramento was destroyed by fire and like most persons, lost everything. From December 1852 to January 1853 Sacramento was under water with the great flood. At this time Winkle was probably "Broke, Busted and Disgusted."

!854 he moved to San Francisco opening a successful bakery on Vallejo & Battery Streets. He stayed in the bakery business until 1871. He then went into the wine & liquor business on the southeast corner of Sacramento & Leidesdorff Streets. Still through all this no mention of a soda business.

However, between 1852 to 1855, Alleman & Stratton were soda manufacturers in Sacramento as well as gold rush towns of Fiddletown and Michigan Bar. They bottled 500 dozen bottles a day, none bearing their name but possibly with Henry Winkle's name.

My theory is that Henry Winkle may have been an early partner or investor with Alleman & Stratton in 1851-1852 and then faced all of the disasters of fire and flood leaving him without funds to continue. Just a thought.

AUGUST WINKLER

Location:	San Bernardino
Face:	**AUG. WINKLER**
	S. B.
	SODA WORKS
Reverse:	Blank
Bottom:	Blank
Rarity:	Rare
Date:	1876 - 1886
Proprietor:	August Winkler
Address:	Third Street
City:	San Bernardino, Ca.
Value:	$ _____

August Winkler is listed as having a liquor and soda factory in San Bernardino from approximately 1876-1883 on Third Street.

In 1883 until his death in 1887 he was listed as proprietor of Winkler's Soda Works. His widow sold the soda works to C. F. Riley.

Aetna Mineral Water	Page 1-2	Empire Soda Works Frank Waldo	Page 86
Aetna Mineral Soda	Page 3	Empire Soda Works E. McG Vallejo	Page 87
American Flag Mineral Water	Page 4	Empire Soda Works Vallejo	Page 88-89
Astorg Mineral Water	Page 5	Excelsior Soda Water	Page 90
Azule Selzer Springs	Page 6	Excelsior Soda & Mineral Water L. A.	Page 91
B (Charles Belden)	Page 7	J. A. Farrell Grass Valley	Page 92
Babb & Co.	Page 8-9	F. M. Modesto	Page 93
Henry Bader XLCR	Page 10	D. L. Fonseca & Co. Jamaica	Page 94-95
John S. Baker Mineral Water	Page 11-13	Fountain & Tallman Calfa	Page 96
Bay City Soda Works	Page 14-15	G. & G. Merced	Page 97
Belfast Ginger Ale	Page 16	J. N. Gerdes S. F. Mineral Water	Page 98-99
The Belfast Ginger Ale Co.	Page 17	Geyser Soda	Page 100
B & G Type 1 Bottle	Page 18	Geyser Soda Springs	Page 101
B & G Type 2 Bottle	Page 19	Geyser Natural Boiled Mineral Water	Page 102
E. L. Billings Sac. City	Page 20-21	Ghiradelli Oakland	Page 103-104
Boley & Co. Type 1 Bottle	Page 22	Golden Gate	Page 105-106
Boley & Co. Type 2 Bottle	Page 23	Golden West Napa County	Page 107
Bonanza Mineral Water	Page 24	Golden West Napa County Nat'l Springs	Page 108-109
Bordwell Mineral Water	Page 25-26	Herve & Somps Natural Mineral Water	Page 110-111
Breig & Schafer	Page 27	Edward Higgins Oroville	Page 112
W. H. Burt	Page 28	Hogan & Thompson San Francisco	Page 113-114
California Seltzer Water	Page 29	Hollister Soda Works A. Mans	Page 115
California Natural Seltzer Water	Page 30	Humboldt Artesian Mineral Water	Page 116-117
California Natural Seltzer Water	Page 31-33	Italian Soda Water San Francisco	Page 118-120
California Soda Works - H. Ficken S. F.	Page 34-35	Jackson's Napa Soda Spring's	Page 121-124
C & K Eagle Soda Works - Sac City	Page 36	Jackson's Napa Soda	Page 125
C & R Eagle Soda Works - Sac City	Page 37	Jackson's Napa Soda Spring's B & Co.	Page 126
Owen Casey Eagle Soda	Page 38-39	Jackson's Napa Soda Spring's Connolly	Page 127
Cassin's English Aerated	Page 40	Jackson's Napa Soda Spring's C. & P.	PAGE 128
C C & B San Francisco	Page 41-42	Jackson's Napa Soda Spring's M. Silva	Page 129
Champagne Mead	Page 43-46	Jackson's Napa Soda Spring's Ed Henry	Page 130
Chase & Co. Mineral Water	Page 47-48	Jackson's Napa Soda Spring's F.M. Vallejo	Page 131
Classen & Co. Pacific Soda Works	Page 49-51	Jackson's Napa Soda Spring's S. & P.	Page 132
Classen & Co. Sparkling	Page 52-53	Jackson's Napa Soda Spring's A. Bresson	Page 133
Columbia Soda Works	Page 54	Jackson's Napa Soda S. F.	Page 134
Columbia Mineral Water	Page 55	Kimball & Co.	Page 135
Columbia R.& H.	Page 56	Lodtmann E & J L	Page 136
Colusa P. & B.	Page 57	B. R. Lippincott Stockton	Page 137
B. F. Connolly Geyser Soda	Page 58	Lippincott & Vaughn Stockton	Page 138
Connolly & Bto. S. F. Geyser Soda	Page 59-61	L. & B. Lippincott & Belding	Page 139
Cross T	Page 62	Littons Mineral Water Healdsburg	Page 140
Crystal Cider	Page 63	Lytton Geyser Soda Springs	Page 141
Crystal Soda Water Co.	Page 64-67	Los Angeles Soda & Mineral Water	Page 142
A. W. Mc Cudworth & Co.	Page 68-71	H. W. Stoll Los Angeles Soda Works	Page 143
W. E. Deamer Grass Valley	Page 72-73	Lynde & Putnam Mineral Waters	Page 144-145
Ditz & Ellerkamp San Francisco	Page 74	M (E. May & Co. Stockton)	Page 146
Delahanty & Shelly	Page 75-76	Martinelli Soda Works Watsonville	Page 147
Eagle Soda Works Sacramento	Page 77-78	McEwin	Page 148
Eastern Cider Co.	Page 79-80	B. J. McGee Benicia	Page 149
El-Dorado	Page 81	B. J. McGee San Francisco	Page 150
Empire Soda Works D S & Co.	Page 82	Merriam's Sonora	Page 151
Empire Soda Works D & M.	Page 83	Millville Glass Works L. M, & Co.	Page 152
Empire Soda Works San Francisco	Page 84-85	Mill's Seltzer Spring's	Page 153-154

Misenheimer & Hall Alma Soda	Page 155
Moise & Co San Francisco	Page 156
Monier & CO. CL FR NA	Page 157
Mooney Visalia	Page 158
M. R. Sacramento	Page 159-160
M. R. & D.	Page 161
Mineral Water	Page 162
Mt. Tamalpais Natural Mineral Water	Page 163
Napa Soda W & W S.F.	Page 164
Napa Soda P & W S.F.	Page 165
Napa Soda Wood's	Page 166
Napa (Star) Wood's (Star) Soda	Page 167-168
Napa Soda Thomas A. White	Page 169
Napa Soda Wood's T.A.W.G.F.	Page 170
Napa Soda Haas Bros.	Page 171-172
Napa Soda Phil Caduc	Page 173-174
Napa Soda Louis Leloy	Page 175
Napa Soda B. F. Connolly	Page 176
Nevada City Soda Works L. Siebert	Page 177-178
New Almaden Mineral Water W. & W.	Page 179-180
A.& P. New Almaden Vichy Water	Page 181-182
New Almaden Vichy Water California	Page 183
New Century Mineral Water	Page 184
New Liberty S. W. Co. (Head) S. F.	Page 185
Neyman & Drake Mok Hill Soda Works	Page 186
Nonpareil Soda Water Co. S. F.	Page 187
Pacific Congress Water (Running Deer)	Page 188
Pacific Congress Water (No Deer)	Page 189
Pacific Congress Water Phil Caduc	Page 190
Pacific Congress Water Sage's	Page 191
Pacific Congress Water Springs Saratoga	Page 192-194
Pacific Glass Works John Taylor	Page 195-196
Pacific Soda Works D. A Mowry	Page 197
F. Paillet Natural Mineral Water	Page 198
Pearson's Soda Works	Page 199
Phillips Napa Co. Soda	Page 200-201
Pioneer (Bear) Soda Water Co. S. F.	Page 202
Pioneer Soda Water San Francisco (T)	Page 203
Pioneer Soda Works PSW in shield	Page 204
Pioneer Soda Works Trade (Shield) Mark	Page 205
Priest's Napa	Page 206-207
Priest's Natural Soda	Page 208
Priest's Natural Soda (Priest figure)	Page 209
Priest Soda Natural (Man)Mineral Water	Page 210
Priest Napa Valley Soda	Page 211
C. A. Reiner's & Co. San Francisco	Page 212-214
Samuel's Napa Spring's	Page 215
Samuel's Napa Spring's A & E	Page 216
Samuel's Napa Spring's A & B	Page 217
Samuel's Soda Trade A Mark Spring's	Page 218
Samuel's Soda Trade M Mark Spring's	Page 219
Samuel's Soda Trade M Mark Spring's S O	Page 220
San Francisco Glass Works	Page 221-222
San Jose Glass Wors (Misspelt)	Page 223
San Luis Obispo Soda Water Works	Page 224
San Rafael Soda Works L. Kapperman	Page 225
San Rafael Soda Works P & B Props.	Page 226
Natural Mineral Water C. Schneer & Co.	Page 227
Somps & Meillette Empire Soda Works	Page 228
P. Somps Mineral Water Napa County	Page 229
Summit Mineral Water J. H.	Page 230
Tahoe Soda Springs	Page 231
Taylor & Co. Soda Water San Francisco	Page 232
Taylor & Co. Valparaiso, Chili	Page 233-235
Asher S. Taylor	Page 236
Tolenas Soda Springs	Page 237
Union Soda Works (Vertical)	Page 238
Vichy Springs Napa Co. Cal.	Page 239-240
Vernon Mineral Water	Page 241
Walter's Napa (Horseshoe) County Soda	Page 242
W & B Shasta	Page 243
Williams & Severance	Page 244-246
Henry Winkle Sac. City	Page 247-248
Aug. Winkler S. B. Soda Works	Page 249

GRACE BROS. BREWERIES, HISTORY & MEMORABILIA
SANTA ROSA - LOS ANGELES – SACRAMENTO - FRESNO

By John C. Burton

With Major Contributions by
Rawley Douglas
John Cartwright
James Arietta
Bob Welch
Cathy Grace-Hayes

LAKE, NAPA, SONOMA, MENDOCINO, SOLANO, MARIN, and HUMBOLDT MINERAL & HOT SPRINGS

By John C. Burton & John Louder
Cover compliments of Witherell Auctions, Sacramento Ca.

SAN RAFAEL - SAUSALITO – SAN ANSELMO
SODA, SELTZER, BEER, AND SPIRITS BOTTLES

A GUIDE AND REFERENCE TO BOTTLERS OF BEER, SODA, SELTZER, AND SPIRITS OF MARIN COUNTY INCLUDING A LISTING OF ANTIQUE BOTTLES

By John C. Burton & John Louder

BOTTLES, TOKENS & HISTORY OF SONOMA COUNTY
May 2017

SODA, BEER, AND WHISKEY BOTTLES
FEATURING SALOON TOKENS

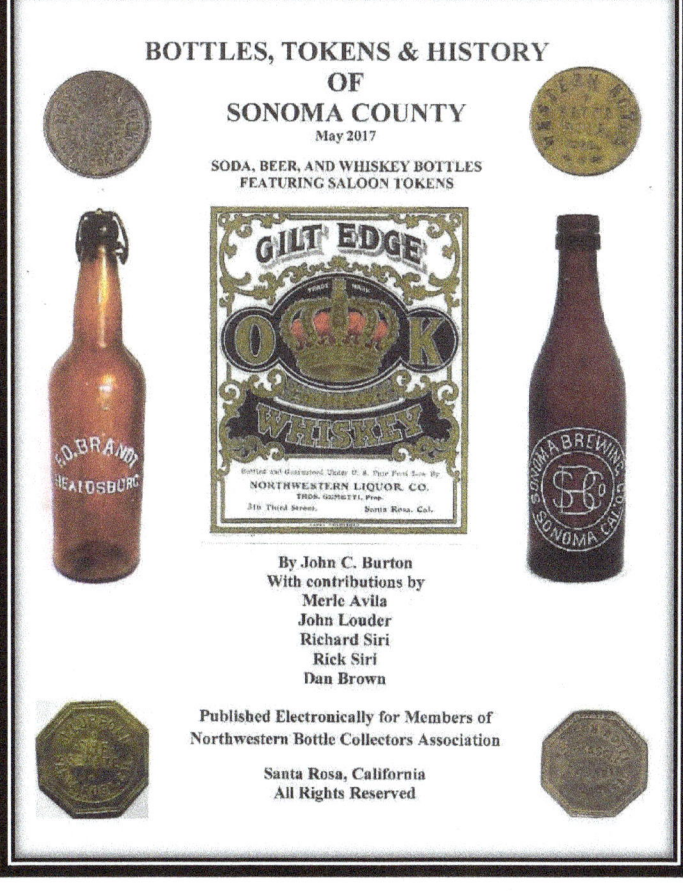

By John C. Burton
With contributions by
Merle Avila
John Louder
Richard Siri
Rick Siri
Dan Brown

Published Electronically for Members of
Northwestern Bottle Collectors Association

Santa Rosa, California
All Rights Reserved

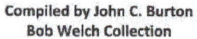

SONOMA COUNTY DRUGGISTS
Featuring Advertising, Bottles, Medicine Glasses, Photographs and Local History

Maynard's Drug Store, Petaluma, circa 1900

Frank A. Sternad and John C. Burton

EARLY MEDICINE BOTTLES OF THE WESTERN FRONTIER

A Guide and Reference of Western Medicine Bottles

Republished by John C. Burton

SONOMA COUNTY BOTTLES, LABELS & BOTTLERS

By John C. Burton

SPLITS & THAT'S IT
A GUIDE AND REFERENCE TO PRE-PROHIBITION
CALIFORNIA HALF PINT BEER BOTTLES
BLOB TOPS, BALTIMORE LOOP & CROWN TOP BOTTLES
By Michael Burgess
Edited by John C. Burton